SCT® IN ACTION

SCT IN ACTION

Applying the Systems-Centered Approach in Organizations

Edited by Susan P. Gantt
and Yvonne M. Agazarian

KARNAC
LONDON   NEW YORK

First published in 2005

Reprinted in 2006 with permission of iUniverse, Inc., New York by
H. Karnac (Books) Ltd.
6 Pembroke Buildings
London NW10 6RE

© 2005, 2006 by Susan P. Gantt and Yvonne M. Agazarian

All rights reserved. No part of this publication may be reproduced, stored in a retrieval system, or transmitted, in any form or by any means, electronic, mechanical, photocopying, recording, or otherwise, without the prior written permission of the publisher.

Trademark Statements:

SCT®, Systems-Centered® and Systems-Centered Therapy® are registered trademarks of Yvonne M. Agazarian and the Systems-Centered Training and Research Institute.

SAVI™ is a trademark of Anita Simon and Yvonne M. Agazarian.

British Library Cataloguing in Publication Data
A C.I.P. for this book is available from the British Library

ISBN: 1855754460
www.karnacbooks.com

Printed & bound by Lightning Source in Great Britain

Contents

Foreword.. ix
    by Ken Eisold

Introduction.. xi
    by Susan Gantt and Yvonne Agazarian

CHAPTER 1   Overview of the Theory of Living Human Systems and its Systems-Centered Practice................ 1
    Susan P. Gantt, Ph.D., ABPP, and Yvonne M. Agazarian, Ed.D., FAGPA, Systems-Centered Training and Research Institute

CHAPTER 2   The Systems-Centered Coach: Examples from Our Work................................... 25
    Frances Carter, LSW, Private Practice, Philadelphia, PA
    Jane Maloney, MA, InterAction Inc., New York, NY
    Irene McHenry, Ph.D., Friends Council on Education, Philadelphia, PA
    Chris McIlroy, MSC, Sandahl Partners, Vaxjo, Sweden
    Caroline Packard, JD, Packard Process Consulting, Philadelphia, PA

CHAPTER 3   Role, Goal and Context in an Organizational Intervention................................. 49
    Verena Murphy, LSW, Consultant, Aurora, OH

CHAPTER 4   From Complaints to Strategies: Using an Agency's All-Staff Meetings as a Learning Lab for Understanding System Dynamics................ 65
    Dorothy Gibbons, LCSW, Consultant, Philadelphia, PA

CHAPTER 5   Opening up the Circle: Next Steps in Group Work for Clinical Pastoral Educators................. 81
    Joan Hemenway, D. Min., Yale University, Guilford, CT

CHAPTER 6   Red, Yellow, Green: Modifying Communication Patterns in an Elementary School System......... 99
     Claudia Byram, Ph.D., Consultant, Philadelphia, PA
     Edward Marshall, Ph.D., Greene Street Friends School, Philadelphia, PA
     Anita Simon, Ed.D., SAVI Communications, Philadelphia, PA

CHAPTER 7   Functional Subgrouping in the Classroom: A Powerful Tool for Learning 129
     Irene McHenry, Ph.D., Friends Council on Education, Philadelphia, PA

CHAPTER 8   Meetings that Work: Making Common Sense "Common" 143
     Beulah Trey, Ph.D., Center for Applied Research, Philadelphia, PA
     Susan P. Gantt, Ph.D., ABPP, Emory University School of Medicine, Atlanta, GA
     Claude Marchessault, MA, Strategic Leadership, New Castle, NH

About the Authors..................................... 163

References 167

Acknowledgements

Our first acknowledgment is to the Management Group of the Systems-Centered Training and Research Institute (SCTRI). We are particularly indebted to the members who have so generously volunteered their time and resources over the last ten years, applying SCT to develop and manage our own organization. This "experiment" has been a live experience of inventing how to manage, and has led us to what we now know about applying SCT to organizations other than our own.

This book has emerged from the work of members of SCTRI who have pioneered SCT methods in the public and private sectors. We want to acknowledge gratefully the work of each of our authors, and also the many SCT members who are represented here in spirit, who have been part of the "trying out" and "thinking through" how to apply SCT to organizational change.

Perhaps our greatest debt is to Kathy Lum for her hard work in assembling and organizing this book and perseverance in finding solutions to the problems along the way. Without her we do not see how we would have had a book! We are also in debt to Dorothy Gibbons for her organization in the early stages which helped us to get going.

And, as always, our personal gratitude to Berj and Kirk who generously supported us with encouragement and understanding throughout the time that it took to make this book a reality.

Foreword

My knowledge of SCT has come about through being asked to consult to the organization that was formed to sustain and develop it, the Systems-Centered Training and Research Institute. My role there has been to help identify the management functions essential to promoting this work and to help develop the appropriate organizational structures to carry them out, consistent with their commitment and values. As a result of working with their Management Group twice annually for about ten years, I have witnessed first hand how SCT approaches making decisions and resolving conflicts.

It has been an astonishing experience. An organization depending entirely on volunteers to do its work, committed to consensus and continual self-evaluation, determined to maintain the highest standards—at the start, I did not know for sure that it could work. And I do not think it would have worked were it not for the power of SCT as a set of methods and procedures for approaching differences, clarifying confusion, and working through conflict.

Having seen some of its best-trained practitioners at work in their own organizational setting has thoroughly confirmed its effectiveness for me. They have consistently managed their differences with intelligence and skill. At one end of the spectrum, the disagreements they have dealt with include problems prioritizing tasks, setting standards for volunteers, planning events, and so forth. At the other end are painful conflicts about setting standards for practice that will inevitably exclude some of those directly engaged in management of the organization or together evaluating competencies for management roles with those currently in those roles. Working ceaselessly at differentiating and synthesizing, identifying disagreements and similarities, they engage in a kind of dance that keeps them working together with their eyes always on the task before them.

The reader coming to this book without direct experience of SCT or training in its methods will, no doubt, have difficulty grasping the particulars of what it looks like in practice or how it works. Such terms as "functional subgrouping" or "person system" or "person in role system," precise as they are to the SCT practitioner, do not easily yield their meaning to the outsider. Nor does this book teach a practitioner how to utilize them. To understand fully how to work with the concepts and methods of SCT, one needs the training that SCT's licensed practitioners provide. Rather than a how-to manual, this book is a collection of preliminary reports from the field, demonstrating its value, and introducing the ideas.

Though its theory of living human systems can be applied to any human system, SCT as the practice was developed initially as a psychotherapeutic procedure for working with groups. Yet as this book amply demonstrates, SCT has turned out to have powerful organizational applications. With its theory of living human systems rather than a separate theory of organizations or of organizational behavior, it uses concepts that easily map onto organizational life. It looks at systems as a whole but also in parts. It stresses the importance of understanding boundaries and contexts. It continually focuses on task, and, perhaps, most important of all, it offers a sophisticated understanding of roles, which includes work roles in organizations.

It well may be, as more consultants working in organizations become more familiar with the concepts and methods SCT offers, the SCT approach will come to seem indispensable to the resolution of conflict.

Ken Eisold
January, 2005

Kenneth Eisold, Ph.D., is a practicing psychoanalyst and organizational consultant. He is President of the International Society for the Psychoanalytic Study of Organizations and teaches in the Organizational Program at the William Alanson White Institute, where he was formerly Director. He has directed the A. K. Rice Institute's National Conference. His writings have focused on the psychodynamics of psychoanalytic institutions, theories of group behavior, and authority in such journals as the *International Journal of Psycho-Analysis, The Journal of the American Psychoanalytic Association, Psychoanalytic Psychology, Contemporary Psychoanalysis, Psychoanalytic Dialogues, Psychoanalytic Inquiry*, and *The Journal of Analytical Psychology*; and in the *Harvard Business Review* and *The Wall Street Journal*. He holds a doctorate in Clinical Psychology and a doctorate in English and Comparative Literature.

Introduction

The systems-centered approach developed by Yvonne Agazarian introduces an innovative orientation to organizations that moves beyond a dichotomy of people-centered versus product-centered companies. Instead, the systems-centered approach focuses on building the living human systems that support the people and the product rather than seeing this dichotomy as only an issue of leadership (Bennis, 1989). Many consultants and managers talk "systems" yet there is a scarcity of know-how for putting "systems" ideas into practice. Systems-centered training (SCT) introduces a human technology for developing systems-centered contexts that increases the emotional intelligence and functioning of the organization itself.

"Thinking systems" brings the kind of fresh perspective that is required for companies to meet the requirements in today's rapidly changing business conditions. Applying systems thinking makes it possible to manage the inevitable challenges that increased diversity brings while continuing to create the innovations necessary not only to survive but also to prosper. It is the system development, more than just the people or resources, that is the limiting factor for how successfully an organization adapts to the far-reaching changes that today's organizations and companies must manage. It is the system development that drives the organizational culture.

The systems-centered approach introduces both a new perspective and an inventive technology: Functional subgrouping is used to resolve conflicts and strengthen decision-making. The systems-centered framework of "role, goal and context" enhances teamwork and lowers personalizing. Deliberately filtering noisy "talk" increases the potential for communication to work. The paradigm of phases of system development in organizations links each phase to specific change strategies.

This collection of articles brings together a range of examples that illustrate these human technologies and applies systems-centered theory and methods to various organizational contexts: companies, non-profit organizations and educational systems. For consultants, managers, teachers, administrators and other change agents, these articles discuss the real-life application of systems-centered methods and the results that can be achieved.

These articles have been written by members of the Systems-Centered Training and Research Institute who are actively involved in applying, refining and developing the SCT applications in organizations.

The first chapter, by Susan Gantt and Yvonne Agazarian, "Overview of the theory of living human systems and its systems-centered practice," summarizes the theory of living human systems developed by Yvonne Agazarian and describes the systems-centered methods and practices that have been developed which apply the theory in organizations.

Chapter Two, "The systems-centered coach: Examples from our work" by Fran Carter, Jane Maloney, Irene McHenry, Chris McIlroy and Caroline Packard, presents five examples of systems-centered methods applied in executive coaching. The authors use sample dialogues to convey both the content and music of the coaching to illustrate how SCT techniques are used in executive coaching.

Chapter Three, "Role, goal and context in an organizational intervention" by Verena Murphy, applies the SCT framework of role, goal and context in a brief organizational consultation. The impact of this framework for shifting a troubled system out of blame and personalizing is detailed and linked to the theory that the framework implements. The example highlights how shifting the frame from a 'problem between personalities' (which frequently results in strong emotions such as frustration and anger) to a role problem opens the way for placing personal experience in the context of the larger environment in which the individuals work. With a decrease in the intensity of emotions, the structural problems in an organization come into focus, and solutions can be reached relatively easily.

In Chapter Four, Dorothy Gibbons, "From complaints to strategies: Using an agency's all-staff meetings as a learning lab for understanding system dynamics," describes the results of a 10-month experiment in functional subgrouping by the staff in one department in a social service agency. With the subgroup system serving as a container for their frustration, the staff members became more energized and curious about the system dynamics that were being enacted in all-staff meetings. As the staff gained a new level of understanding of system dynamics, they developed more effective strategies for participating in all-staff meetings and for negotiating the agency's bureaucratic system.

Chapter Five, "Opening up the circle: Next steps in group work for clinical pastoral educators" by Joan Hemenway, describes the introduction of SCT into pastoral education. Because joining and leading groups is a ubiquitous part of local faith communities, it is the responsibility of pastoral educators to make fuller use of the process group experience in their educational programs. The systems-centered approach to group work is particularly appealing to educators for at least five reasons: 1) it integrates a number of psychological understandings in its theoretical approach; 2) it focuses on system-wide dynamics rather than on individual personalities; 3) its practice retains an educational framework (participants as learners) rather than a therapeutic (participants as patients) framework; 4) its methods and language are accessible and appealing even to those with no specific psychological training; and 5) its focus on exploring information in feelings in the here-and-now, and being curious about the unknown, is important territory for pastoral educators in their group work.

In Chapter Six, "Red, yellow, green: Modifying communication patterns in an elementary school system," Claudia Byram, Edward Marshall, and Anita Simon conceptualize an elementary school as three subsystems: administration, faculty, and students. The system goal is to develop students' range of intelligence. In this chapter, they trace the path of an intervention introducing a communication technology (SAVI: System for Analyzing Verbal Interaction; Simon & Agazarian, 1967) to each system level and track its impact on the ability of the system to move towards its goal on all system levels.

Chapter Seven, "Functional subgrouping in the classroom: A powerful tool for learning" by Irene McHenry, describes an action research study which introduced functional subgrouping as a tool for deepening learning in academic contexts. The school groups were from different educational levels: young adolescents in a middle school, older adolescents in a high school, adult students in a master's degree program, and a faculty team in a doctoral program. The findings suggest that functional subgrouping is an effective tool for deepening student understanding of academic content, for engaging students at an emotional level to enhance their cognitive learning, for developing listening skills, and for engaging students in a meta-cognitive process during a class discussion. Functional subgrouping was also effectively used as a method for dialogue in a faculty development seminar.

Chapter Eight, "Meetings that work: Making common sense 'common,'" by Beulah Trey, Susan P. Gantt, and Claude Marchessault addresses the invisible system forces that govern meetings. This article describes how to use SCT methods to structure meetings that produce results that are creative, reality-based, and sound. Dividing meetings into three segments, the challenges and structures necessary at each phase to ensure productive and efficient meetings are identified and the SCT techniques used are described.

These chapters cover a range of applications that represent the SCT methods and the systems thinking that underlies SCT practice. The diversity of the chapters is an asset in learning to think systems instead of just people. Since introducing systems ideas may be a relatively different perspective for some readers, we suggest "a willing suspension of disbelief" in reading this book in order to try out the systems way of thinking and doing to see if it shifts your thinking and ways of doing.

Susan Gantt
Yvonne Agazarian
January, 2005

1

Overview of the Theory of Living Human Systems and its Systems-Centered Practice

Susan P. Gantt, Ph.D., ABPP
Systems-Centered Training and Research Institute
Yvonne M. Agazarian, Ed.D., FAGPA
Systems-Centered Training and Research Institute

This chapter introduces the theory of living human systems developed by Yvonne Agazarian (Agazarian, 1986, 1993, 1997; Agazarian & Gantt, 2000) and its systems-centered methods for organizations and work teams (Agazarian & Philibossian, 1998; Gantt & Agazarian, 2004). A theory of living human systems (TLHS) provides an umbrella theory and a way of thinking that can be applied with any living human system, and its systems-centered methods for organizations are used by leaders, managers, consultants, educators and organizational members.

A theory of living human systems built on and integrated much work from other theorists in the field, most especially, Lewin's (1951) field theory, von Bertlanffy's (1968) general systems theory, Miller's (1978) systems theory, Shannon and Weaver's 1964) mathematical theory of communication, Howard & Scott's (1974) theory of stress, Korzybski's (1948) general semantics, and Bennis and Shephard's (1956) theory of group development. Building on these theorists, Agazarian (1992, 1997) has offered an integrative theory for understanding living human systems (the developmental journey is described in Agazarian & Gantt, 2000). Perhaps most importantly for organizations, TLHS and its systems-centered methods introduce a human technology that provides specific influence strategies that introduce a systems orientation into organizations.

Systems thinking is not a new idea in the organizational world. Senge (1990) is perhaps the most influential writer to call for the importance of organizations moving toward systems thinking. In spite of the excitement that Senge's ideas introduced, the lack of operational definitions for his ideas has made it difficult to translate them into practice. In contrast, the systems-centered practice derived from Agazarian's theory of living human systems (TLHS) translates the theory into operational definitions with the methods and techniques that put it into practice.

Thus, TLHS makes it possible not only to introduce methods that move organizations towards a systems approach but also to introduce systems thinking as a norm. Perhaps, particularly significant is the systems-centered training (SCT) protocol that makes the idea of emotional intelligence trainable at the different levels of an organization: its members, its different departments and work groups as well as the organization as a whole (Gantt & Agazarian, 2004). SCT moves systems thinking out of the world of ideas and into the world of Work.

Central to SCT is the understanding that organizational behavior is more heavily influenced by the system that has been developed in the organization than it is by any of the individuals who are working within it. When fully understood, this seminal idea has the potential to move us beyond the person-centered culture which dominates most organizations to a systems-centered culture. Recognizing that the system is the governor that both sets the potential for individual behavior and experience, and frees organizations from the implosive effect of personalizing, opens new pathways for formulating change strategies.

The implications of this are very important. When a work team understands its work from a systems perspective, not only are the members of the team less likely to take their work and each other so personally, but they are also more likely to be freer to raise questions or ideas as information for the group rather than suppressing, or expressing, them for personal reasons. When the context is systems-centered rather than person-centered, members learn to take "citizenship" in the organization as well as in their departments and work groups and to raise the kind of questions about a company's research or accounting practices that "citizens" raise as part of their organizational role. This makes for a very different organizational culture.

The rest of this chapter introduces a theory of living human systems (TLHS) and an overview of the systems-centered methods for organizations.

The Theory of Living Human Systems

The theory states: "A theory of living human systems (TLHS) defines a hierarchy of isomorphic systems that are energy-organizing, goal-directed and self-correcting" (Agazarian, 1997). Making this statement user-friendly starts by defining each of the terms so that it is clear what each term means and how it is being used. It then becomes possible to test these ideas in the real world of people. Testing these ideas led to the systems-centered methods (Agazarian, 1997; Agazarian & Philibossian, 1998). Since the ideas came first and implementation second, SCT is a theory-driven practice. Each systems-centered intervention functions as a hypothesis that tests the validity of the theory and the reliability of its practice.

Learning to think about systems and not just people may be the biggest challenge for human beings. This process is greatly facilitated by the illustration of a circle (we are all much less likely to personalize a circle than ourselves or another person). A circle can represent a system, the organization as a system, or a department as a system, or a work team as a system or a classroom as a system.

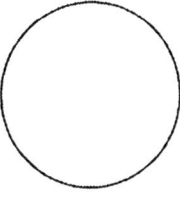

Figure 1

Hierarchy

The term hierarchy is familiar to those who work in organizations. Yet, systems hierarchy has a different meaning from an organizational hierarchy. Organizational hierarchy relates to the formal organizational structure and the lines of authority, accountability and responsibility and is part of any systems organizational structure. Systems hierarchy introduces context. Thus, it does not matter which position on the organizational chart is under consideration, whether it be a department or a management team or a role. A systems hierarchy will observe the system in context—existing as a "middle" system within the context of the system above it, and serving as the context for the system below it.

Figure 2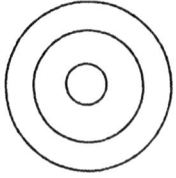

In figure 2, the middle circle exists in the context of the larger circle and the middle system is the context for the smaller circle. Thus, in applying hierarchy to an organization, the larger circle can represent the department, the middle circle can represent the work teams in the department, and the smaller circle can represent the roles in the work teams. Each of the circles is itself a system. Or similarly, the larger circle can represent upper management; the middle circle, middle management; and the smaller circle, the line staff. Most important of all, at whatever level in the hierarchy these three systems exist, each system is itself a system governed by system properties as defined by the TLHS.

The middle system. Drawing the three circles to illustrate hierarchy led to the simple yet radical understanding that the middle system in a hierarchy of three systems is the most efficient focus for a change intervention for the whole system (Agazarian, 1992; Agazarian & Janoff, 1993). The middle system has adjacent boundaries with both the larger system context and the smaller system for which it provides a context (see figure 3). Making a change to the middle system has an immediate potential impact on both the larger system and the smaller system within it.

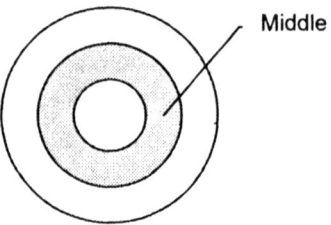

Figure 3

The implications of this are revolutionary. Let us assume the change goal for the whole system is the color "gray," as illustrated in figure 3. Putting gray into the middle system will have the biggest "bang for the buck" as the middle system has a direct influence on both the larger system and the smaller system. See figures 4, 5, and 6.

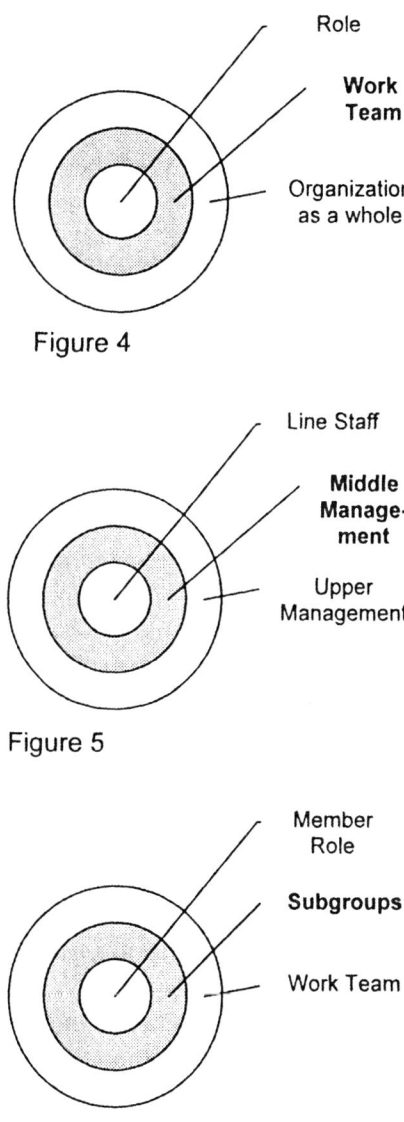

Figure 4

Figure 5

Figure 6

Not only does a system always exist in a hierarchy of systems, any particular system can also be viewed in terms of system hierarchy. For instance, if we apply the idea of hierarchy within a work team, the work team is the larger system, the middle system is the subgroups that develop as the team works (that can either be functional or stereotypic) and the smaller subsystem consists of the roles that members take (see figure 6). From this perspective, the subgroup as the middle system is the most efficient place to influence change in the team. As change occurs at the subgroup level (middle system), the change influences both the work team as a whole and its members. Influencing the subgroup system so that it is functional rather than stereotypic is the heart of the systems-centered approach. A functional middle system serves as the nexus of stability and change.

The middle system and functional subgrouping. Applying this understanding about the middle system to groups led Agazarian to developing the method of functional subgrouping which enables the integration of differences by making boundaries permeable. By influencing change in the middle system of a work group, functional subgrouping then influences the work group as a whole and its members. Functional subgrouping is used in work teams for resolving conflicts and decision-making (Agazarian & Philibossian, 1998) and provides an important alternative to stereotyped subgrouping. Stereotype subgrouping maintains differences behind closed boundaries. In organizations, stereotyped subgrouping is often based on status hierarchies. Introducing the alternative of functional subgrouping shifts to exploring the relevant rather than stereotyped differences in a conflict or decision in a way they can be integrated in the service of the work. For example, exploring in alternating subgroups, the competing energies in a work group of "wanting to move ahead" and "wanting to slow down," allows both points of view to be integrated in the work group. By making it possible for the information in both points of view to be explored, functional subgrouping interrupts the human tendency to contend over or try to convert differences.

Context. Hierarchy orients to context. In figures 4, 5, 6, and 7, the larger circle is the context for the middle circle, which in turn is the context for the smaller circle. Seeing an organization or a work team in its context (Agazarian & Philibossian, 1998; Gantt & Agazarian, 2004) clarifies the realities of what is and is not possible. This has had a big impact on the people in the organizations in which we work. Strategic planning and decision-making has a very different orientation when managers and leaders and consultants work with an understanding of context. Context includes the realities of an organization, the impact of these organizational realities on the people within it, and the impact of the organization on its larger context. When the people who work in organizations recognize that the difficult realities relate to the larger organizational context, and even the larger community or world context, their relationship to those realities shifts.

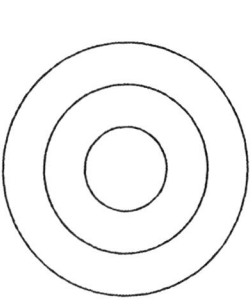 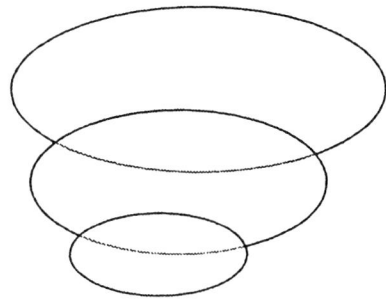

Figure 7

Target system. Understanding that a change strategy impacts not only the system that is directly changed but also the systems above and below in the system hierarchy leads to taking three systems into account in any change strategy. SCT refers to any three nested systems in a defined hierarchy as the "target system for change." Orienting to the target system highlights an intervention's sphere of impact not only on the system where the change is directed (the middle system) but also on the systems above and below it. Identifying the target system for change then links the change goals to context (Gantt & Agazarian, 2004). This understanding influences how change strategies are designed. Once the target system for the change goal is identified, a change strategy can be mapped that maximizes efficiency by intervening to the middle system of the target system.

Exporting change to other contexts. Another practical application that relates to systems thinking is the recognition of how important it is that the neighboring systems in a system hierarchy be addressed if the changes in the middle system are to be supported within the larger context (Agazarian & Philibossian, 1998).

For example, in a mid-size company, a work group changed its norms from a "fast action" approach to "exploring for information" before action (look before you leap!). This change worked quite well *within* the work group. Then members of the work group took this change to other contexts in the organization: as they attended other meetings, they began asking the other groups to "stop and think" first before taking action. The other groups found this disruptive and deviant from their usual working style. The new behavior was discouraged and soon work group members became reluctant to use their new behaviors. The consultants recognized that their consulting work, though successful within the team, was being discouraged in other contexts. Recognizing their error, they then refocused the original work group on how to communicate the change into the other contexts so that they could be heard. When members paid deliberate attention to <u>how</u> to export new norms across the boundaries, the change became integrated as part of the company's working style.

The SCT framework of role, goal and context. Another important emphasis developed from applying the idea of systems hierarchy is the SCT framework of role, goal and context (Agazarian & Gantt, 2005). Every system is a context in which work is done. Every context has a goal. And every context requires specific roles from its members to enable the system to move towards its goals. Thus it is an operational step to think about the definitions of role, goal and context of the specific system under analysis. For example, in our own organization (the Systems-Centered Training and Research Institute), we have a number of work groups. Each of these work groups is a context with a defined goal. Let us use the Membership Work Group as an illustration. This group has the goal of maintaining and increasing membership. Within the group, there are defined roles that orient to this goal, and roles like new member coordinator and membership benefits coordinator. Each of these roles can then be defined by functional behaviors that link to the goals of the work group.

Role, goal and context as an alternative to personalizing. SCT works with teams to identify their context, clarify the goal of their context, the roles in the context and how each role links to the goal. This introduces a significant orienting perspective to a work team and provides an important alternative to personalizing. In a work group, for example, when a member of the work group is designated to take on the role of keeping the group on track, other members are less likely to take personally the frustration of "task" role interruptions; whereas, if the same member speaks up without the authority of the role, it is easy to react both personally and resentfully. When personalizing is lowered, it is easier for a work team to work.

Changing contexts and roles. Similarly, as members explicitly identify the array of contexts in which they work, and the goal of each context, they are able to identify the role changes they make as they change contexts. Sometimes there is an intuitive understanding of how to change one's behavior, as when someone shifts from the role of member in the executive team meeting to a leader in the sales meeting. It is intuitively obvious that as the goal of the context changes, so does the role. Identifying and making these role shifts explicit, makes it easier, not only for the person to deliberately change behavior to fit the role but also for those relating to this person to relate differently and to avoid treating the "leader" as a member, or the "member" as a leader.

Using the force field to strengthen role and team performance. Once the role is clear, SCT works with a team and its members to identify a force field of specific behaviors that implement the roles. Agazarian (1986; Agazarian & Gantt, 2000) adapted the force field from Lewin (1951). A force field identifies the forces that move toward a goal (driving forces) as well as those forces that move away from its goal (restraining forces). For example, the force field below represents the driving and restraining forces for the role of a team leader where the team has the goal of marketing a new product.

Role of Team Leader Driving Forces → ← Restraining Forces	
Clarifying the goal →	← Being vague about the task
Interrupting to orient back to task→	←Bringing in tangential issues
Asking for ideas→	← Monopolizing, interrupting new ideas

Figure 8

In figure 8, the force field identifies the specific role behaviors that support the goal of the context (driving forces) and provides a behavioral map for supporting and enhancing role performance. Most important, the force field identifies the behaviors that disrupt the goal orientation (called restraining forces). Lewin (1951) demonstrated that decreasing restraining forces in a change process is more effective than trying to increase driving forces. This orientation to change is fundamental to SCT strategies for change. Reducing restraining forces automatically releases driving forces. In addition, when the restraining forces are weakened in a change process, it induces less tension and stress than when the driving forces are increased to stimulate change (Lewin, 1951).

SCT uses the force field for diagnosing an organization at any system level. In the example above, an SCT manager or consultant would also work with the team to identify the force field of the driving and restraining forces for team performance. A force field provides a map of behaviors that can be weakened (restraining forces) to strengthen goal orientation (see figure 8).

Goal alignment within systems and across systems. SCT, building on Bridger's (1946, 1990) understanding of the importance of clear goals, emphasizes goal clarity at every system level. In addition, SCT highlights the issue of alignment between roles and the goal of the specific context. Within a context, if the role behaviors do not align with the goals of the context, very little progress will be made toward the goal. Thus, aligning role behaviors towards the goal is a driving force.

Another driving force is alignment of the goals of a subsystem with the larger system goals. For example, it is important for departmental goals to align with organizational goals. Aligning goals across system contexts within an organization enhances system functioning.

Goal alignment is also relevant to an organization in its larger community context. If the organization's goals are not in an alignment with the community goals, either the organization's resources will be restricted or the community goals sabotaged. When an organization aligns its goals with its community goals, the organization can be thought of as taking its citizenship in the community to support the goals of the community context. Citizenship is closely related to what SCT calls "member role."

Member role in the team. The idea of role is not new in organizations. In fact defining roles as related to function is widespread. It is common in many work groups to have various work functions represented in work roles: for example, marketing, finance, research or acquisitions. SCT introduces the idea of "member role" in a work team as an added dimension in understanding role. Before one can take on the responsibility of being a member, one must first select from one's personal resources those that are relevant to membership. The emphasis on "member role" orients works group members to the work group and the goal of the context. As work groups begin to understand the idea of member role different from function roles like marketing or finance, they often report feeling much clearer about how to take part in the meetings when an unfamiliar area is being discussed. For example, one member reported: "I feel much freer now to ask questions now that I see that my questions help all of us to clarify, and that clarifying is part of my member role and useful to the group's work."

When the member role is clear, then it is much easier to align the function role (i.e., marketing) with the member role; this also aligns the function role to the goal of the context. People then learn how their function role changes as they change context and are able to identify simple changes to make in their behavior as they change contexts. For instance, the marketing representative learns to select the marketing information about a new product she brings into a meeting, dependent on the context she is in. With her own marketing team, she is much more detailed in her presentation. With the global product work group, she orients to the bigger picture and vision.

Orienting to member role in a work group also develops the kind of understanding that makes it possible for members to begin to recognize that subgroups in a group have a role for the group. For example, in a work group focused on revising its strategic plan, several members reported being bored. The "bored" subgroup interrupted its impulse to withdraw and re-oriented itself to discovering what role it had for the work group in the discussion of the strategic plan. They identified the importance of working on a strategic plan that they could feel excited about and noticed that their withdrawal was a signal that the excitement was missing. This recognition re-kindled interest in the group, and the group was then able to work with much more energy towards a strategic plan.

Clarifying the member role, which requires identifying the behaviors that contribute to supporting the goal of the context, enables another important role discrimination. Clarity about member role brings into focus the difference between the driving forces of goal-related role behavior and the restraining forces of personalizing roles around personal goals. Identifying the force field for member roles provides a working map for the team to use both in orienting their work together, and for getting back on course when pulled off.

Isomorphy

We next turn to another aspect of the theory. TLHS links hierarchy with *isomorphy*. Building on von Bertanlanffy (1968), TLHS defines *isomorphy* as similarity in structure and function of systems in a defined hierarchy. Practically, this means that understanding the organizational structure and function at any one system level gives you information about the structure and function of every other system level in the hierarchy.

Just as hierarchy enables a clarification of the relevant context for targeting change strategies to meet change goals efficiently, isomorphy makes it possible to see the interdependence of every system and subsystem in the system hierarchy. For example, "leaping before you look" was characteristic of all levels in the organization we described earlier. To be successful in making an organizational change towards "looking before you leap" required the change be integrated at every level of the organizational hierarchy.

Structure and function are interdependent aspects of system isomorphy. Structure relates to how the information crosses the boundary into a system. Function relates to how information is organized within a system. Structure will be discussed first followed by a discussion of function.

Structure and Boundaries

TLHS defines *structure* in terms of boundaries. Boundaries demarcate what is in a system and what is outside it. When using the illustration of a circle to represent a system, the line of the circle represents the boundary. The permeability of boundaries determines when information comes into or out of a system. Open systems have relatively permeable boundaries to information (figure 9). Closed systems have relatively impermeable boundaries (figure 10).

Figure 9   Figure 10

Thus defining structure as boundaries leads to looking at the boundary permeability between and within subsystems, and the degree to which a system is open or closed to information. For example, it is useful to assess whether the boundaries within a work team are open or closed to its members bringing in information, or whether one work team is open or closed to giving and getting information from another work team.

Boundary permeability. The issue of boundary permeability can be elaborated by returning to our earlier picture of three concentric circles and the idea of introducing the change of "gray" into the system. Using our understanding of hierarchy, we wanted to introduce "gray" to the middle system first (see figure 4). The boundary permeability of the middle system to "gray" will be relevant in introducing this change. Also, how we influence the boundary from the middle system to the larger system and from the middle system to the smaller system nested within it so that the change crosses the boundaries in both directions of the hierarchy will also relate to boundary permeability. Understanding boundary permeability is essential in communicating information or transferring change from one system to another as well as within a system.

SCT identifies two conditions under which boundaries close (Agazarian, 1997; Agazarian & Gantt, 2005). Boundaries close to noise in communication and also close to differences that are too different for a system to integrate (Agazarian, 1989). Thus the more noise in a communication, defined as ambiguity and redundancy (Shannon & Weaver, 1964), and contradiction (Simon & Agazarian, 1967), the more the boundary closes to information. In addition, communications that introduce differences that are too different from the current system organization will also stimulate boundaries to close.

Clarifying when boundaries are too open or too closed requires being clear on the goal. When the goal is transferring information from one system to another, relatively open boundaries will facilitate information transfer. When a system is consolidating or integrating a change, relatively closed or impermeable boundaries to further change information will facilitate the goal of integration.

Filtering "noisy" talk. SCT influences a work group or organizational group to filter noise out of the communication process by introducing techniques for changing ambiguous, vague communications to specifics, changing redundancy to the "bottom line," and changing "yes, but" contradictions by teaching members to join on similarities before introducing a difference. When noise is filtered out of "talk," boundaries become more permeable to information.

The goal of communication is to transfer information across boundaries. Thus, when communication works, "talk" (written or oral) provides fuel for work. When the boundaries are closed inappropriately, an intervention is necessary. Many SCT interventions are based on SAVI (Simon & Agazarian, 1967). SAVI, the system for analyzing verbal information, was developed as a method of identifying entropic and neg-entropic communication patterns and provides an operational definition that integrates Shannon and Weaver's (1964) communication theory and Howard and Scott's (1974) theory of stress.

The SAVI model for communication training provides an easy-to-learn template for organizations and work groups to use to identify and change noisy communications. SAVI identifies the communications that contribute to work as green light, those that interfere with work as red light and those that are contingent on the overall communication pattern as yellow light behaviors. Identifying red, yellow and green behaviors serves as a practical guide to members as to *how to* modify a noisy communication climate and filter out noisy communications so the boundaries can open to information.

Function

TLHS defines *function* as the process by which systems survive, develop and transform through discriminating and integrating differences, differences in the apparently similar and similarities in the apparently different (Agazarian, 1997).

The issue of integrating differences is crucial in organizational functioning. Like any living human system, organizations tend to stabilize around sameness and close their boundaries to difference. Though this is a reality of human systems and not personal to people, people tend to personalize their own and others reactions to differences. Recognizing this reality as a universal for all human beings, makes it easier to establish norms for normalizing and managing the inevitable challenge of managing conflicts and differences.

SCT identifies the ability to manage conflict and differences as essential in an organization's functioning if the organization is to continue to develop and change. To the extent that differences can be integrated, organizations shift from avoiding or contending over differences to integrating them as a resource. This is particularly important in today's climate of rapid change and an ever-increasing diversity in the work force. More and more, companies that do not update their business models find that the changes in market conditions are such that their viability is threatened. Opening to new ideas is a significant driving force for innovation and change while the human pull to repeat the past and resist the new is a restraining force to change. Companies are faced with the challenge of simultaneously maintaining enough of the stability of what works while integrating new ideas. For example, in a recent newspaper article, one troubled company was described as being noted for their "unhealthy tendency to avoid candid internal debate on business issues" (Kempner, 2004). Stories abound of teams producing bad decisions and losing their common sense, or of discouraging team members from bringing in dissenting viewpoints. Sandberg (2004) cites Edmondson's (1999, 2002) three barriers to good team functioning: 1) team members do not recognize the information they have as relevant or interesting and then do not share it, 2) team members do not recognize that there are opposing viewpoints, or 3) members withhold information.

SCT introduces the innovative method of functional subgrouping for managing differences and resolving conflicts. Functional subgrouping reduces the barriers to effective team functioning. When differences are more easily integrated in functional subgrouping, team members learn to see their communication as information for the team and are less likely to judge it or withhold it.

Functional subgrouping. SCT introduces functional subgrouping as a conflict resolution tool that facilitates the discrimination and integration of differences. In a work team or meeting, members are trained to join and explore their similarities with others who have a perspective similar to theirs. This interrupts the human tendency to convert or extrude or personalize differences. Instead, first one subgroup explores one aspect of a difference together, while the other subgroup holds. When the first is ready to hold, the second subgroup works. As each subgroup explores in a climate of relative similarity, each subgroup discovers the differences within their subgroup in what was initially similar. In a climate of relative similarity within each subgroup, these discovered differences are more easily tolerated. At some point, both subgroups begin to discover the similarities in what was initially different between the two subgroups and integration happens in the group-as-a-whole. The simplest introduction to functional subgrouping is to encourage the phrase, "anybody else?"

> Tom: I want us to get going today and really get our ideas about a strategic plan into writing. I am impatient. Anybody else?
> Sue: Yes, I am too but I am not clear yet about what our ideas are. Anybody else?
> Consultant: That is a "yes, but" which signals we have two subgroups, one representing, "being not clear," and the other representing "wanting to move ahead." Who is in which camp so far?
> Jon: I am not clear today and I was clear last time.
> Kiki: I don't feel ready to move fast yet, so I am closer to not clear.
> Sue: I don't think I am clear enough to move ahead, anybody else?
> Jon: I want us to see where we are before we move ahead, like where we left off.
> Consultant: So we have two important camps, one camp where the job is to clarify. The other side with energy to move ahead. Is anyone else in that subgroup as well?
> Sally: I am, I am ready to get it done!
> Consultant: So which subgroup does the group want to support working first?
> Sally: I would support the clarifiers as I think getting clear first will help us get our work done.

As work groups learn the norms for functional subgrouping (join on similarities, ask "anybody else" after your contribution, and hold differences until the first subgroup pauses), members learn to see that every subgroup is a part of the whole. Subgroups in a work group are like the offensive and defensive squads of a football team; both squads are important to the overall team performance and both play a role for the team. Learning to take one's role in a subgroup orients the team and its members to systems thinking and weakens the restraining forces that Edmondson identified: judging one's contributions as irrelevant or uninteresting, failing to recognize opposing viewpoints, or withholding information. Functional subgrouping also fosters an atmosphere of innovation in that differences begin to be seen as potential resources.

The method of functional subgrouping has been used successfully both for conflict resolution and decision-making in organizational work groups (Gantt & Agazarian, 2004). A preliminary study (Parks, 2003) suggested that stranger teams trained in functional subgrouping for 30 minutes prior to the experimental work task were quicker to arrive at a decision and evidenced less conflict than those given 30 minutes of ice breaker training. Others (McHenry, 2003; Parks, 2003) have introduced functional subgrouping in classrooms and have discovered that subgrouping helps to facilitate a good climate for learning while providing the students with a structure to explore issues more thoroughly.

Energy

All living human systems need energy contained by structure in order to function. As mentioned earlier, borrowing from Miller (1978), SCT defines energy as information. SCT describes information as including both the comprehensive information (observable data and facts) and the apprehensive information (intuitive knowledge). It is the capacity to integrate these two kinds of human knowledge, the comprehensive and the apprehensive, that SCT identifies as underlying emotional intelligence in work groups and organizations. For example, a work group may report strong accomplishments from the preceding work quarter, yet the lack of energy in the tone says something very different. Getting clarity on the information contained in the tone is as important as getting the numbers and is even more relevant for the team's current and future functioning. Tracking system energy in an organization always gives a useful picture of a system's functioning.

Energy-Organizing

SCT looks at how a system organizes energy in terms of its ability to discriminate and integrate information. Discriminating and integrating information is the process by which living human systems survive, develop and transform from simpler to more complex. This defines system function at the theoretical level.

System development is relatively easy to describe. A new idea comes into a work group. It is initially met with much hesitation (the status quo seems like survival). As those who are hesitant explore their hesitations, followed by those who are interested in the new idea, the work group develops a more complex understanding of both sides and starts to discover the common ground between both sides (survival moves toward development). System transformation happens when a work group is able to do things it could not do before. For example, in a board that had been meeting over several years, the board regularly groused about being over burdened with details yet the board members continued to bring in details from their areas of expertise and to spend their time discussing these details. The board recognized the problem but for several years was unable to change it. Changing this behavior required a transformation in how the board worked. At the most recent board meeting, the board had actually transformed in how it worked (not its membership!) and was able for the first time to address issues of policy and vision.

Practically, how a system manages differences and conflicts influences how the system functions and transforms itself. To the extent that a system organizes itself so that differences are avoided or kept out, there will be limited potential for the creativity and innovation so critical in today's rapidly changing market conditions. In contrast, integrating differences increases emergence and "thinking outside of the box."

Goal-Directed

Energy can be directed toward or away from system goals. SCT identifies both the primary and secondary goals that operate in living human systems. The secondary goals are the stated tasks or the explicit goals the group formed to do. Primary goals on the other hand are inherent in all living human systems: to survive, develop and transform from simpler to more complex (Agazarian, 1997). The extent to which the primary goals are being met determines the amount of energy available for the secondary goals. Similar to Bridger's (1990) idea of "double tasks" in a group, SCT emphasizes the importance of focusing on primary and secondary goals in enhancing system functioning.

Another discrimination about goals has also proved useful, the difference between the explicit and implicit goals in secondary goal orientation. [Bion (1959) did the pioneering work that highlighted the difference between what a group says it is doing and what it actually does.] The explicit goals are what a group says it is doing. The implicit goals are those that can be inferred from group behavior. When SCT consultants collect a force field with a work group, the data of the force field can be used to infer the group's implicit goals. In the example below (figure 11), the implicit goal that can be inferred from the restraining forces is fight. The driving forces imply a goal of integrating differences and acknowledging frustration. The data of more restraining than driving forces suggests that the group energy at the current time is more related to fighting over differences.

Work Group Force Field	
Subgrouping around differences→	←Yes, but's and arguments
Identifying frustrating realities→	←Scapegoating and blaming
	←Outrage and malicious gossip

Figure 11

The SCT consultant or manager would work with this team to identify and weaken the "easiest to weaken" restraining force. Weakening the restraining force frees the driving forces for integrating the differences.

In the example above, identifying the implicit goals makes it possible to see where the group is in relation to the primary goals of survival, development and transformation. An implicit goal of flight or freeze is, strangely enough, more related to survival, while fight is more related to development. Applying this to work groups, flight and freeze move away from work whereas fight contains conflict, which when resolved, releases the energy for work.

Phases of system development. Building on the work of Bennis and Shepard (1956), SCT organizes a sequence of the phases of system development. SCT identifies phases of authority, collaboration and interdependent work as inherent in all living human systems (Agazarian & Gantt, 2003). Each phase represents a developmental goal in the service of the system's survival, development and transformation from simpler to more complex. Each work group has to manage its developmental challenges in each phase. In the authority phase, with its subphases of flight, fight and role locks, a work group has the challenge of developing a problem-solving orientation, learning to build a working relationship with the leadership and taking one's authority to do one's role. In the collaboration phase, the challenge is to work collaboratively with each other using the differential resources of the work group members. In the work phase, the challenge is to bring one's energy and resources into one's role with an awareness of goal and context.

The idea of phases of development is not a new one. Wheelan (1994/2004) provides an excellent review of the wide-ranging models of group development, many of whose stages are quite similar to those used by SCT. What SCT introduces that is new is seeing each phase of development as a system: a goal-oriented system, with a structure and function characteristic of the system phase. SCT then identifies the force field that links to the primary goal orientation of each phase. Thus, SCT identifies a force field of behavioral manifestations for each specific phase of development.

This force field of each phase of development then makes it possible to diagnose the phase orientation. Simultaneously, the force field for each phase serves as a map for identifying which restraining forces to weaken. Weakening the relevant phase-specific restraining forces releases both the driving forces for development as well as releases the energy for work. The chart below illustrates the predicted force field for each of the phases:

Figure 12

FORCE FIELD OF DRIVING AND RESTRAINING FORCES IN THE PHASES OF SYSTEM DEVELOPMENT	
FLIGHT FROM THE PRESENT	
Explore→	←Explain
Learn to subgroup by saying "anybody else" → at the end of message (systems- centered)	←Personalizing communications and remaining self-centered
Exploring wish to be given care→	←Creating an identified patient role
Giving care in response to genuine care seeking→	←Asking to be taken care of or Care taking (dominant/submissive role relationships)
Reality Testing →	←Negative Predictions and mind reads
FIGHTING OVER DIFFERENCES	
Subgroup around differences→	←Saying yes-but; monologues disguised as a dialogue;
Joining the scapegoat and exploring similarities→	←Scapegoating
ROLE LOCKS WITH EACH OTHER	
Entering into the member role in context and→ working towards the goal of the context	←Repeating old interpersonal roles,
Recognizing the source of the role and → discriminating between past and present	←Role induction and Role suction.
ROLE LOCKS WITH AUTHORITY	
Seeing the larger picture as the context for→ frustration with inner and outer authority	←Personalizing, blaming leader or self
Co-operating with outer and inner authority→	←Reacting with defiance or compliance
COLLABORATION	
Developing good relationships based on → cooperating with leader and each other for work	←Competing rather than working together
Earning work rewards→	←Expecting reward for just being oneself
Taking on the appropriate work role in the → context and working towards the goal of the context	←Personalizing. ←Working within personal roles with personal goals and ignoring the context.
WORK AND PLAY	
Putting one's heart into work, play → and relationships	←Working and playing without commitment:
Using one's common sense in → relationship to the larger picture	←Following the letter of the law and not the spirit ←Failing to recognize the larger picture
Using both one's apprehensive and → comprehensive information for solving problems (emotional intelligence)	←Following only one's comprehension, or only one's apprehensive intuition for solving problems

Yvonne M. Agazarian, © 2004

For example, in the flight phase, as a work group or organization weakens negative predictions, it is able to collect data and reality test, as a foundation for developing a problem-solving orientation. This moves the system toward its next phase of development and simultaneously frees energy for reality testing that can be used in its organizational work.

For most organizations and work groups, working with the phases of fight, role locks with each other and role locks with authority are the most challenging of the phases. In the fight subphase, SCT uses functional subgrouping, which has proven especially useful in that it reduces the tendency to scapegoat or attack difference. When work groups learn to use functional subgrouping as an alternative to fighting, the work group learns to contain frustration. This provides an important foundation for the challenges of learning to weaken the personal role inductions with colleagues or the tendency toward compliance or defiance with the team leader. For example, a middle manager in a coaching session recently recognized that his most important challenge is to shift from sabotaging by either opposing or complying with his direct report in the company to finding an effective way to work with the leader he has. Once he recognized this as an important professional challenge for him, he was able to shift from being preoccupied with resentfulness toward his direct report to experimenting with how to work effectively with him and the realities of his leadership style.

SCT technique for choice: Fork in the road. The issue of goal orientation in organizations and work groups is an important one throughout the phases of system development. SCT introduces the "fork in the road" of choice with work groups to help the group to clarify its goal orientation and to direct its energy toward its goal. [Theoretically, this relates to vectoring energy, borrowing from physics, in that a vector has a direction (a goal orientation), a point of application (a target), and velocity (an energetic force). The SCT adaptation of the force field presents driving and restraining forces as vectors which determine the equilibrium of a system for that moment in time.] SCT consultants and leaders not only use the force field but also introduce the fork in the road to orient a work group to identify how much energy is available for which direction and to make a clear choice about where to put its energy. For example, asking a group to clarify whether it wants to work on the vision of its strategic plan or the implementation details helps a work group to organize its energy toward a clear goal. In the coaching example above, the middle manager began to recognize the "fork in the road" between sabotaging his direct report and recognizing the professional development challenge of learning to work with him.

Self-Correcting

Living human systems self-correct through regulating the amount of information/energy that enters the system. By closing to differences that are too different for the system to integrate, or to noise that interferes with information transfer, living human systems maintain and self-correct. Too much noise or difference disrupts system function. Thus, boundaries open or close as a process of self-correction. When system boundaries close, the system corrects itself by becoming relatively impermeable to the differences the system is not yet able to integrate. System boundaries open to new information when it is similar enough to integrate. Thus self-correction of boundary permeability maintains the energy flow to support system survival, development and transformation. Leaders and managers influence this self-correction process by filtering noise out of communication and introducing functional subgrouping for managing differences.

Putting It All Together

Using the SCT theory and methods enables consultants, managers, leaders and educators to see a work group or organization as a living human system. The development of the living human system inherent in an organization governs the organizational potential, that is, the system has more to do with how personal resources are used than the people themselves. Thus, if we want more emotional intelligence in organizational members, we must create living human systems that are more emotionally intelligent (Gantt & Agazarian, 2004). The heart of emotional intelligence is learning to use both cognitive and intuitive information/energy in context. Rather than taking an organization just personally, the organizational realities can be clarified and strategies developed that take the reality context into account.

Systems assessment. Seeing an organization as a living human system also enables a systems assessment that focuses on system components rather than just people. Asking questions that focus on the system variables identifies the influence of the system context on human behavior. An organization can then be assessed in terms of the system variables.

Some of the important questions that orient an SCT consultant or manager are as follows:

- What is the relevant system hierarchy for the goal of this consultation? What is the target system for change?
- How much of the communications are characterized by contextualizing versus personalizing?
- Are roles clear and oriented to goal and context?
- Are the boundaries appropriately permeable between departments? How clear are the boundaries that contain the work of each department?
- Are the boundaries appropriately permeable within the organizational teams and work groups?

- How open is communication?
- Where the communication flow is restricted, which boundaries are open and which are closed? Is the boundary appropriately permeable for the goal of the context?
- How do differences get managed? Is innovation high in this company?
- What is the emotional intelligence of the organization? How much of intuitive knowledge is supported?
- What is the phase of system development characteristic of the company? And of the departments within it?

Emotionally intelligent organizations. SCT orients to the emotional intelligence of living human systems rather than focusing on emotional intelligence as a property of an individual (Gantt & Agazarian, 2004). This shift implements the systems-centered understanding that the system sets and limits the potential for organizational functioning more than the individual resources per se. Thus systems thinking can be used to identify the system conditions that potentiate emotional intelligence at all system levels, the organization as a whole, its work groups, and its roles.

SCT methods. SCT introduces an array of methods that provide a human technology for influencing living human systems. These methods make it possible not only to implement a systems attitude and orientation in organizations but also to provide an orientation for consulting and problem-solving that orients to system solutions rather than personnel solutions. The specific SCT models provide practical strategies for intervening and influencing organizations in ways that foster the development of the living human systems. Specifically, SCT introduces the following:

- functional subgrouping for conflict resolution and decision-making so that differences can be used as resources to support innovation rather than divisiveness
- a model for clarifying role, goal and context so that behavior can be oriented to support the goal of the context at all system levels
- methods for filtering communications to open or close boundaries to decrease noise and increase information flow

- a way of identifying the target system so that change interventions can be implemented in context
- the map of the phases of system development with identifiable force fields for diagnosing and intervening to work groups and organizations
- contextualizing as an alternative to personalizing

Yet most important of all, TLHS and SCT introduce methods and models that enable an organization to adopt a systems orientation without compromising its goals. SCT methods promote emotional intelligence at all system levels in the organization. The developmental potential for all living human systems is to learn to move beyond the dichotomous orientation of "us and them" to taking up our membership to contribute to the system and in turn be influenced by the system to which we are contributing and influencing, in an ongoing process of self-centering in a systems-centered context.

2

The Systems-Centered Coach: Examples from Our Work

Frances Carter, LSW, Private Practice
Jane Maloney, MA, InterAction Inc.
Irene McHenry, Ph.D., Friends Council on Education
Chris McIlroy, MSC, Sandahl Partners
Caroline Packard, JD, Packard Process Consulting
Contributing Editor: Richard O'Neill, Ph.D.

This chapter provides five case examples showing how systems-centered theory and methods were used to structure leadership development in an executive coaching context. Dialogue excerpts illustrate how systems-centered coaches work with their clients to help direct system energy toward its goals. The case examples illustrate how systems-centered coaches translate the language of systems-centered protocols for undoing restraining forces (Agazarian, 1997) into everyday workplace language for use in an organizational context. In all cases, the coaches work to increase the client's awareness of choice and capacity to choose: choice of role, choice of behavior, choice of communication.

In these examples, a school principal regains energy for his work; a chief executive officer learns to help his executive team to cooperate with each other in planning an effective meeting by clarifying roles and goals, a sales support manager uses the connection between her loss of energy and the frustration she feels towards her organization to improve her department's effectiveness; a middle manager learns to create a plan for resolving a conflict between himself and his supervisor; and a school principal learns to undo an anxious thought that has kept him from giving effective negative feedback to his staff.

A Theory of Living Human Systems and Systems-Centered Coaching

A theory of living human systems states that all systems are goal-oriented and that there is an innate system drive towards the primary goals of survival, development and transformation and the secondary goal of environmental mastery (Agazarian, 1997). A system-centered coach's job is to work with leaders as they develop their organizations by setting goals and helping organization members focus energy on the goal. In this process, the systems-centered coach supports the leader in creating clarity of role, goal and context, and in developing relevant communication and action.

The systems-centered approach equates energy with information (Agazarian, 1997). With this simple definition, SCT focuses the second phase of the consultation (once a manager or leader has set goals) on exploring and improving the flow of information and patterns of communication that enable the organization to put goals into action.

Executives usually seek coaching because they are interested in developing their leadership skills; are concerned about their job performance or the performance of those they supervise; are feeling a loss of energy or motivation for work; or are unsure how to resolve interpersonal conflicts at work. The systems-centered protocols for undoing anxiety, tension, and depression (Agazarian & Philibossian, 1998) are especially valuable in coaching work, because of their brief, clear, and sequenced step-by-step skills a client can learn. The case studies with illustrated coach-client dialogue demonstrate the translation of systems-centered language into everyday workplace language for use in an organizational context.

A systems-centered approach to coaching also means being able to appreciate the importance of thinking in terms of different perspectives. The particular perspective from which we view a problem not only creates the ramifications for the problem itself but also influences the solutions that we may find in trying to solve it.

A systems-centered coach starts a consultation by asking questions about roles, goals and contexts, trying to identify just where the problem is. These questions would be what SCT calls *Contextualizing* interventions. Secondly, the coach would help the client to make connections between the different contexts, the different roles and the different goals.

The third part of the consultation would be helping the client focus his or her energy on what he or she can do and directing energy and resources away from all the things that are distracting or a drain on energy and resources. The final part would be a combination of *Boundarying* interventions, which reduce noise in the system to keep irrelevant information out, and *Vectoring* interventions that redirect energy towards goals and away from distractions.

In the following pages of this chapter we hope that you will be able to get a feel for how systems-centered coaching works in the real world of different organizations, small working groups and individual managers. We feel sure that you will be able to appreciate the power of being able to apply different perspectives to a problem where before there was only one. By changing perspectives, it becomes possible to utilize the potential of every client to find choices and to make decisions about which role suits which goal in which context.

The Challenges for Executive Coaching

Executive coaching is starting to emerge as a profession. Between 1993 and 2003 the number of published theoretical and empirical peer-reviewed papers on coaching increased threefold (Grant & Cavanaugh, 2004). Coaches and clients have reached a point in which they are becoming aware of the value of basing their work on a "solid theoretical understanding" and moving away from "one size fits all" coaching models (Grant & Cavanaugh, 2004).

The theory of living human systems and SCT methods provide an integrated theory and methods for developing individual, team and organizational capacity to achieve goals. Before the development of the theory of living human systems, coaching consultants and organizational consultants could draw upon psychological theory or organization theory. The two theories offer different ways of understanding and assessing the functioning of a client system. Psychological theory focuses primarily on the individual. Organizational theory focuses on the structure of the organization. Consultants could choose one of the two theories. Consultants who wanted to draw on individual and organizational perspectives could shift back and forth between two different ways of framing the consultation.

Consultants trained in TLHS have a framework that integrates both perspectives. Systems-centered training (SCT) makes the connection between the theory and intervention. When a coach applies development methods that are based upon the same theory that was used to assess the functioning of a system, the coach can assess and refine the development process as it unfolds. The coach consultant that is equipped with the theory of living human systems and "hands-on" SCT methods can create the optimal pace and sequence of learning that is appropriate to the client's stage of development and builds from the simplest skill to the more complex.

SCT also makes the connection between the individual and the organization. The individual is seen in his or her context as a member of an organization. A coach using SCT assumes that the member's voice is speaking for a subgroup within the organization. (All interventions are thought of as a voice for the organization.)

Overview of Systems-Centered Coaching

Every coach who participated in writing this chapter came to coaching from a different background ranging from education, clinical psychology, organizational development, business, social psychology and social work. Despite our diverse training, we discovered that our use of SCT enabled us to help our clients achieve results more effectively and with less effort. Each of us found that SCT and its theory of living human systems provided a meta-theory that has enabled us to assess functioning, set goals and apply our diverse skills to move the client toward success.

The International Coaching Federation (ICF, 2005) defines professional coaching as "an ongoing professional relationship that helps people produce extraordinary results in their lives, careers, businesses or organizations. Through the process of coaching, clients deepen their learning, improve their performance, and enhance their quality of life."

The ICF code of ethics promotes coaching that honors the client as the expert in his/her life and work, believes that every client is creative, resourceful, and whole (ICF, 2005). This ethical stance aligns well with systems-centered theory and practice. The case examples in this chapter demonstrate how coaches stayed within the role of coach as defined by the ICF by using systems-centered techniques to guide clients in discovering and clarifying solutions while staying responsible and accountable to their leadership goals and values as well as the organization's goals and values. The cases demonstrate the following:

- The systems-centered coach-client interaction fosters clarity—clarity of role, goal, communication, and action.
- The systems-centered coach-client interaction increases the client's awareness of choice: choice of role, choice of behaviour, choice of communication.
- The systems-centered coach assists the client in focusing on present reality and what the client is willing to do to achieve a goal.
- The systems-centered coach assists the client to weaken their internal restraining forces and the system restraining forces that are relevant to weaken in order to move forward toward the goals.

- The systems-centered coach assists the client in clarifying the lines of authority, accountability and responsibility.

Look for the following systems-centered techniques in the cases that follow.

Clarifying roles, goals, and context (Case Examples 2, 3, 4).
Identify driving and restraining forces toward specific goals (Case Example 4).
Getting out of worry mode and into curiosity mode (Case Examples 1, 4).
Undoing loss of energy by identifying sources of suppressed frustration or anger (Case Examples 1, 3).
Containing and exploring frustration or anger as a source of energy and information (Case Examples 1, 3).
Recognizing and shedding old habitual roles, and develop new roles that further organizational and personal goals (Case Example 4).
Directing energy and information-flow in ways that further a broader range of organizational goals (Case Examples 3, 5).
Using functional subgrouping to resolve conflicts (Case Examples 2, 5).

Case Example 1: Using the SCT Protocol for Undoing Depression: A School Principal Learns to Find New Energy in Unexpected Places

Michael is in his first year as the principal of a small elementary school. He began the year with high energy and vision. When he called to request a consulting session with an SCT coach, mid-way through the year, he said he was exhausted and feeling like a failure.

At the beginning of the session, the coach could see that Michael's energy was very low. He had a list of complaints, primarily about the faculty. He complained that they did not trust him and were not working to implement the changes that he was trying to make for the good of the system. The first intervention by the coach using SCT methods was to guide Michael into a thorough description of present reality by asking for the facts of the situation and separating the facts from the feelings generated by the facts. In this process, the coach helped Michael to bring his awareness to the present reality, which allowed him to undo many negative predictions about the future, thus decreasing his anxiety about the future. The coach pointed out to Michael that he was "mind reading" what other people were thinking of him and his work. The coach made suggestions for reality checks on several of these mind reads. This early work in SCT coaching, the undoing of negative predictions and the reality checking of mind reads shifts the client into a reality—testing mode and problem-solving orientation.

Noting that Michael's overall energy was still quite low, his body posture and affect were despondent, and that he did not report any tension, the coach selected a systems-centered framework that would help Michael to discover the trigger for his loss of energy and then work to set reality-based goals for systemic interventions. The coach adapted the systems-centered protocol for depression into language appropriate for the principal's context in order to support him in systematically undoing his depression.

By following the step-by-step directions of the coach through the protocol sequence, the principal was able to realize the energy of his anger and use it to mobilize himself into action. Here is a reconstruction of their exchange, based on the coach's notes from the conversation, at the point where the protocol use begins.

> Coach: Are you feeling a lack of energy?
> Michael: Yes, no energy at all. I am always exhausted. There is too much to do, and I cannot seem to make any progress.
> (Next, the coach uses the SCT technique of focusing Michael on finding the bracket of time in the past that contained the loss of energy, as a way of finding the trigger for the depression.)
> Coach: When is the last time you remember having lots of energy?
> Michael. In November, at the Thanksgiving feast that the older students prepared for our Thanksgiving party.
> Coach: When did you first notice this loss of energy?
> Michael: I remember that I thought I could hardly make it through December until the winter holiday break. I was very glad to get out of school, but issues weighed heavily on my mind throughout the vacation period.
> Coach: What happened in between the Thanksgiving party and the beginning of winter holiday break that might have triggered this loss of energy?
> Michael: Well, at the December board meeting, the board was critical of several items in the proposed budget that I had worked on with the business manager.
> Coach: Was that when you first noticed the loss of energy?
> Michael: No, I think it was after that. I think it was on the last day before the vacation when students and faculty left early (noon dismissal) and actually, now that I think about it, only one person from the faculty stopped by my office to wish me a happy holiday. I was just sitting there in my office by myself in the afternoon and no one else stopped by. In particular, Mrs. Baker, the most senior teacher with whom I have been trying to build bridges, just walked past my office door and out of the building without saying anything to me.
> (Continuing with the SCT protocol, the coach inquires about the feeling linked to that moment in time. Feelings of frustration and anger, when not

fully experienced can be turned inward against the self, resulting in a loss of energy).
Coach: How did you feel when you noticed her walking by the door and leaving the school without wishing you a happy holiday?
Michael: Well, I felt a little like, "Oh well, so much for that."
Coach: What feeling went with the thought: oh well, so much for that?
Michael: I was a little bit angry, but also I figured that it doesn't matter that much to me whether she talks to me or not.
Coach: Can you recall that little bit of anger right now?
(Bringing the feeling fully into the body in the present will support Michael in regaining his energy).
Michael: Yes, now that you mention it, I think I was really pissed off at the time.
Coach: Let yourself fully feel your anger right now and tell me what you notice about the anger.
Michael: Ah, that feels better. Yes, you were right. I was really very mad because...
Coach [interrupting]: The "because" doesn't matter right now. Just feel the anger and frustration of that moment. Describe the feeling of anger to me.
(In systems-centered work, it is essential to keep the client focused on exploring all aspects of an experience, rather than rationally explaining it. Exploring at the apprehensive level, rather than explaining from a familiar comprehensive perspective, brings new information into the person system. This new information makes the client's own creative life energy available to him).
Michael: Hot belly, tight jaw, seeing red. Like I am on the football field ready to charge.
Coach: Sometimes when we miss a moment of anger and don't feel it fully, then it gets turned inside ourselves like a boomerang, and that can result in a major loss of energy.
Michael: I didn't know that. Yes, I can see that now. I think that is what happened.
Coach: Are you feeling more energy now?
Michael: Yes, I feel stronger.
Coach: What do you think got in the way of your feeling the full anger in the moment when you first noticed Mrs. Baker walking out the door without saying anything to you?
Michael: I think I do not allow myself to feel anger in general. I think that I should be able to take whatever comes and not get riled up about it. I tell myself some things don't matter when, in fact, they do matter to me.
Coach: Do you see that taking a moment to fully notice and feel your feelings, especially feelings of irritation, frustration or anger, can energize you? You don't have to act upon anger—just have the energy in it.
Michael: Based on what we talked about today, I am going to experiment with this idea and practice fully noticing and feeling my anger.

The coach continued in the coaching role with Michael for the rest of the academic year. During these sessions, Michael reported that he was noticing more often when he was irritable or angry, and he did not return to a state of despondency. He learned to value the energy that came from recognizing the anger, rather than turning it inside. The image he frequently used was the image of himself on the front line in a football game, at the line, ready for the game to begin, full of focused energy and strength that he could then apply to his work.

Case Example 2: A CEO Learns to Help his Executive Team Cooperate with Each Other to Plan an Effective Meeting Through SCT Coaching that Focused on Clarifying Roles and Goals, Undoing Negative Predictions and Using Functional Subgrouping for Conflict Resolution

This CEO of "Artrix" (the company names used here are fictional to provide anonymity for the companies involved), a highly innovative technology company, sought coaching to prepare for work with his executive team. He was angry and frustrated with the members of this team. The team was getting good reviews from clients about the company product itself, but negative feedback on their communication style during meetings. Clients reported that team members were vague, interrupted and contradicted each other, and expressed agitation and frustration by tapping their fingers, getting up and down repeatedly, moving around the room, gesturing behind clients' backs. One client told Ambrose that this team was "shooting itself in the foot," and some clients were expressing reluctance to work with the company as a result.

At the time of the consultation, "Artrix" and "The Customer Company" were equal competitors in the industry in one context and The Customer Company was a subcontractor to Artrix in another. This CEO was working with a representative from The Customer Company to present Artrix for acquisition by the larger company. The CEO was planning to bring this team together for a presentation and he wanted his team to perform well.

Coaching the CEO: Undoing negative prediction and containing the impulse to retaliate. The first step in this consultation was to work with the CEO, using the SCT technique to undo his negative predictions (Agazarian, 1997), contain his anger and retaliatory impulse and bring his energy into the present for planning and feedback. When energy and focus is tied up in the negative prediction, the affect is generated from thoughts or interpretations rather than data in reality, and the force of the prediction can stimulate behavior that can bring about a self-fulfilling prophesy. In the work of undoing a negative prediction, reality testing is encouraged, feelings in relation to the reality are contained and energy is freed up for planning.

> CEO: I am really distracted. I am so angry with this team. Yesterday, in a meeting with another client, I actually saw Dennis (SVP of Marketing) tapping his foot, making faces and getting up and pacing around the room, and handing notes behind the client's back to Pamela (another member of the team). I know they are going to sabotage the meeting with The Customer Company!
> Coach: You are angry with the team and Dennis.
> CEO: Yes, everyone was distracted by the behavior, I still am.
> Coach: There are two parts to it, your anger about yesterday and the prediction that this will happen in the meeting later in the week.
> CEO: Yes.
> Coach: Let's look at the concern you have that Dennis will "sabotage" the The Customer Company meeting. Can you be more specific about what you actually mean when you say "sabotage?"
> CEO: Yes, I think he will not be focused, contradict other team members, distract everyone else, and annoy the client.
> Coach: When you think about the upcoming meeting that way, how do you feel about it?
> CEO: I am furious.
> Coach: And when you are this furious, what happens?
> CEO: I just want to bash him and everyone. I lose my focus, lose my sense of the goal and that's not good. Unfortunately, I can't fire him, we need him.
> Coach: Can you see that some of the fury is actually coming from how you are thinking about it, the negative prediction that Dennis will not be focused, will contradict others and the client will be annoyed?
> CEO: Yes.
> Coach: Can you actually predict what is going to happen in the future?
> CEO: No, not really
> Coach: Do you have any way of knowing how Dennis will handle himself in the meeting?
> CEO: No, not really, we haven't planned yet.
> Coach: When you stop there, and sit with the unknown, what's that like for you?
> CEO: I am still angry but more controlled and I have more energy. (The CEO paused) I know we (the Coach and CEO) have our meeting with the team and I can give Dennis feedback before then. I feel more focused, on the goal again, my role and I can see more options. Ready to get to work.
> Coach: Then let's look at the second part. Do you have a plan and context for giving Dennis feedback on his behavior?
> CEO: We have an Executive Team Meeting Tuesday and we can review yesterday's meeting. I can let him know what I saw and how I felt.

Coach: Feedback as information without irritation?
CEO: [laughs] Yes.
Coach: How is it to have a clear plan for giving feedback?
CEO: I am more focused and ready to get this team working.

Clarification of context, goal and role. Using the concept of hierarchy and the SCT method of contextualizing makes it possible to understand complex business relationships, to develop strategies and goals and to make interventions in a business climate where in one context one might be partners and in another, competitors.

In planning for a major company initiative, the coach worked with the CEO to clarify the different role relationships between her company and the client company. Each role relationship or subsystem has its goals related to the context. By mapping the different contexts, different goals and different subsystems, the CEO was able to be clearer about the upcoming meeting.

Clarifying the context and goal of the initiative with the CEO. In this intervention, the consultant worked with the CEO to establish the context for the upcoming meeting with a company where there are many overlapping role relationships. As the CEO was in preliminary negotiations for the potential sale of the company, and the meeting with a current competitor, he was concerned they would ask for financial information he was not prepared to disclose. This planning would determine what information belonged in the presentation and what information belonged to other working contexts. Prior to the work with the whole team, the Coach worked with the CEO to get clearer about the overall goals of this company initiative and the role of this presentation within that context.

Coach: What is the purpose of this presentation?
CEO: The Customer Company wants to send a technical team down to see what we do and what we have.
Coach: What is your goal for Arttrix in having them come down? (Clarify the goal at the Company-as-a-whole level.)
CEO: Well, my goal is to sell the company or to partner with The Customer Company.
Coach: Is this a shared goal?
CEO: It is between us, but our contact says his technical people aren't convinced.
Coach: So how would you formulate the goal of this presentation?
CEO: To shift his technical team from "no" to a "yes."

Coach: Who in your organization are best suited to participate in this presentation? (The Coach is identifying both a functional role and the resources needed for the role.)
CEO: My technical team—Our Chief Technical Architect, Engineering, Chief of Clinical. (This clarifies which subsystem within the Company as a whole is most functional for participation in the meeting, given the goals.)
Coach: For the presentation itself, do you know the actual concerns to be addressed in the meeting?
CEO: He sent an email saying his tech people don't see how we are any different from an EDC (electronic device company). They want to make sure our technology will interface with theirs, and to make sure it doesn't just end up on their shelves.
Coach: If we start with the actual information in the email, it sounds like there are three specific restraints they would like to address at this stage. Can your team prepare to address them?
CEO: Yes. Our Chief Technical Architect can address the differences, Engineering can address compatibility issues and Head of Clinical can address the relevance. I am much clearer now. If they want financial information, we can take another step later.

Consulting to the CEO and executive team: Functional subgrouping as a conflict resolution technique. Next, the consultant worked with the CEO and the executive team to plan the presentation. The SCT consultant's role during this phase of work was to facilitate the planning process, support the CEO and coach the team to use clear, exploratory and problem solving communication.

In meeting with the executive team, the CEO, building on the coaching described above, presented the company response for each area at this stage. The team responded with differences of opinion, a 'yes-but' communication pattern and a flurry of negative predictions:

"I think we should just wing it; we don't know what they really want."

"But, I think we need to make a plan."

"Yes, but we don't want to sound artificial or scripted."

"They are going to use this information against us and bad-mouth us in the industry."

Each member built a "case" for their own opinion, based on speculations and interpretations.

The SCT consultant interrupted the arguments and the communication pattern, supported the energy in the group, and legitimized the impulse to react or attack differences. The consultant stressed the importance of differences for any group and its problem solving process and introduced functional subgrouping as a technique for resolving conflicts (Agazarian & Philibossian, 1998) that helps a group use its differences to develop its potential.

The instruction for functional subgrouping was a simple set of steps: 1) after speaking, ask "anyone else?" 2) If you have a similar point of view or feeling, join and add your own piece 3) look at the people you are talking to 4) if you have a difference, hold on to it, wait until there is a pause and ask if there is room for a difference. There will be time for all sides to talk.

Two subgroups developed. One subgroup focused on the importance of not using a "script" that might make the presentation seem artificial or stiff, and would risk being unresponsive to the actual interests of those attending. The concern was in wanting to avoid being preoccupied with the "letter of the law" and losing the "spirit and connection." The other subgroup wanted to develop a strategic approach to the presentation, ensuring that it would touch on the relevant issues, with content that all team members could support. The concern focused on the fear there would be too much ambiguity and the team would contradict each other in the attempt to "fill in the gaps." As the two subgroups worked, they were able to listen to each other and come together around keeping the spirit inside the strategic approach. The whole team was on board for planning the structure and general content of the presentation, while recognizing the need to "read and respond" to the actual people when they arrived. This "integration" of the two subgroups allowed the natural conflict between spontaneity and planning to be contained and explored. All members were able to see and experience the benefits of both, their energy was contained and free and they were able to direct this energy toward the planning and problem solving.

Building the presentation structure and delegating leadership. As the energy in the team was now free, work with the structure was accomplished quickly, problems were solved creatively and there was excitement and joking among team members.

In planning the presentation, the SCT consultant worked with the team to build a structure with clear boundaries and clear roles that related to the goals of each aspect of the presentation. The overall time frame for the day was established, the agenda was set and areas of content were organized into specific sections. Each section had a clear goal and a designated leader assigned based on their area of expertise. As each section was planned, the team clarified where the backup resources were and how to use them. One member of the team was also assigned the responsibility of keeping an eye on the "big picture" and another for watching the "nuts and bolts." The team also attended to the geographical boundaries, locating rooms, planning for flow from one room to another, and identifying necessary equipment and materials. As the clarity in structure developed and functional role responsibility clarified, the team's highly efficient and professional behavior was restored.

Outcome. The CEO and his executive team learned to: define the context of a presentation, clarify the goals and assign explicit leadership roles strategically using resources and expertise of all members. The team learned to plan the flow of a meeting, delegate leadership within the sections of a presentation, think through specifically who will say what and how, and harness their energy for work. They learned how to reduce the "noise" in their communication and to explore an issue rather than argue over differences of opinion. The executives learned to reduce the ambiguity around the goal and their roles, and to clarify the lines of authority when coming together as a presentation team. As the work progressed, there was less frustration, irritability and competition, and more free energy, cooperation, collaboration and creativity. After the presentation, the client company's feedback was, "The team really went up a notch, worked together better than I have ever seen."

Case Example 3: Using the SCT Framework for Clarifying Roles, Goals, and Context: A Sales Support Manager Makes the Connection Between Her Loss of Energy and the Frustration She Feels Towards Her Organization, and She Learns to Work with Her Supervisor and Manager to Clarify Roles, Goals, and Context

Isabelle was referred for consultation with an SCT coach by her HR manager because of a loss of energy she had been experiencing for the last six or seven months. She had returned to work after maternity leave eight months earlier, had been feeling listless and tired, and had begun to question her abilities as a manager. She was very unhappy about the way things were at her workplace. She felt she had not succeeded in her role as manager despite all her efforts and all the energy she had put into making the new department work and making her colleagues feel valuable and worthwhile in their roles. There was conflict and disagreement between Isabelle's department and the supply department.

The coach helped Isabelle make connections between her role and responsibilities within the context of her own department and also in relationship to the supply department and its manager. Making the connections also helped her find out more about what her responsibility was and wasn't.

Coach: Do you think you have more or less authority than the supply manager to make decisions about the way his supply department works with your sales support department?
Isabelle: But I have to make it work.
Coach: Is the supply department your responsibility?
Isabelle [*pauses; suddenly smiles; her face lights up*]: I have thought about talking to both the supply manager (Ken) and the purchasing manager (Richard) about my problems. I realize I don't have the power to tell the supply department how they should work together with his department, but maybe I should be able to do it anyway.
Coach: Is it reasonable to expect that from yourself, when you don't have the actual authority to do it?
Isabelle. [Another smile]. No.
Coach: Could your tiredness in some way be caused by all the energy you are using trying to resolve working relationships between the two departments?
Isabelle: Yes. I feel it's my responsibility to make things work.
Coach: In your department you have a responsibility to make things work. Okay. Do you see that you don't have the authority to make things work in Ken's department?
Isabelle: Yes, I can see that. I have been trying to get members of the supply group to work with us by cajoling, arguing, and charming them. I haven't tried to work out the different responsibilities between Ken and me. I will talk first to Ken and then to Richard about clarifying their roles.
Coach: Can you picture how the organization would function if you were on the same level as Ken? Would that make a difference? And if so, is it a difference that would be more or less functional for the business area?
Isabelle: It would be much clearer for everybody, and it would be easier to work out agreements between myself and Ken. It wasn't a problem in the beginning. It seemed okay to me that Ken was my boss, because my department is so new, and we've never tried this kind of organizational structure before.
Coach: You said earlier that you don't feel much energy anymore, is that correct?
Isabelle: Yes. I've been feeling really, really tired for the last seven or eight months.
Coach: Do you feel that way at home too with your daughter?
Isabelle: Oh, no! Patricia is so full of life, and I can't wait to get home and pick her up from the daycare center.
Coach: So it depends on the circumstances or the context you are in whether or not you feel tired or not?
Isabelle: Yes, it does. I feel dread when I open the front door of my office building.
Coach: What are you dreading?

The Systems-Centered Coach 39

> Isabelle: I'm afraid that some of my staff will come and tell me how badly things are going and how agreements aren't being kept by the members of the supply department.

The coach focused on undoing a number of Isabelle's anxiety provoking negative predictions using the techniques previously described in case example #1. Isabelle was then able to shift her attention and resources from worrying about the future to open curiosity. The focus of the consultation also shifted to roles.

> Coach: Okay. You mentioned earlier that you have been trying very hard to resolve conflicts between some members of your department and some members of Ken's department, was that correct?
> Isabelle: Yes. It has been a real drain, and I've been thinking that maybe I'm not suited to be in this new role in this new department anyway. We have a meeting set up for next week when both our departments will have whole day to discuss how we've been working together so far.
> Coach: Really? That sounds like good timing. Who was it that arranged the meeting?
> Isabelle: Well, it was me.
> Coach. And what do you see as your role at that meeting?
> Isabelle. Well, I think I should explain to the supply department how our department has felt during the last year.
> Coach: And if you take up the role of being a lightening rod for your department how do you think the members of the supply department will react?
> Isabelle: What do you mean lightening rod?
> Coach: Well, you will in effect be transferring the opinions of your department to the members of the supply department, causing a bit of thunder, don't you think?
> Isabelle: Yes, they probably won't like it, but what else can I do? I have to try and make them listen to us, don't I?
> Coach: It would be best if they did listen; that's correct. I don't think you can make them listen, do you?
> Isabelle: Okay, so what can I do then?
> Coach: Do you think that Ken might have the same idea about the meeting that you have, voicing the opinions from the different department members?
> Isabelle: He might.
> Coach: So if you both take up the role of lightening rod, as I called it, how long do you think that either department will listen to the other one?
> Isabelle: No, all right, that's probably not the best strategy. I can see that.

Outcome. Isabelle arranged to meet with Ken and discuss how the different departments had been working together during the previous year. She was also able to discuss the role of lightening rod that each of them had held for their departments and to find more useful ways of structuring the meeting in accordance with the goals that both Ken and she had. The coaching sessions continued for a few months, and Isabelle became more aware of a number of personal roles that she automatically took up. She then explored the type of roles she could instead develop that were more appropriate to the needs of the department and the organization as a whole. Her energy returned and she felt more worthwhile in the role of manager.

Case Example 4: Undoing Anxiety: A School Principal Learns to Undo a Pattern in Which Parents' Complaints Send Him into an Anxious, De-skilled Mode that Keeps Him from Giving Effective Negative Feedback to His Staff

Ted, the head of a small independent school, asked a systems-centered coach for help interrupting a difficult dynamic among his teaching staff. Some of the teachers were feeling hurt and demoralized by other teachers who were habitually criticizing their teaching styles and methods. The coach noticed that Ted's perspective on the problem was almost completely people-centered, rather than organizational. He was describing the problem as if it had to do with how to avoid hurting people's feelings. He was not looking at the problem from the organizational perspective of how to do effective performance management. In systems-centered terms, Ted was missing an understanding of the full context in which the problem was occurring.

Systems-centered theory predicts that when a client sees a problem not just as a "people" problem but also as a specific kind of organizational dysfunction, and clarifies his role in supporting the organization's improved functioning, he is better able to discover a solution to the problem. The coach therefore began by using the systems-centered technique of "contextualizing," designed to help the client make the connection between the goal of the context he is in, and his role in supporting that goal. She asked Ted whether the school had a formal performance management process. Ted responded that there was no such process. He was initially defensive about this, another sign that he was personalizing and not yet seeing things in context. The coach therefore used the SCT technique of normalizing, again to expand his sense of context and shift him out of personalizing.

> Coach: It makes sense that your school hasn't had a formal performance management process until now. Many small organizations don't have a formal process until they start to grow. Your school is now beginning to grow, and

therefore you are starting to need a more formal process. So you are right on schedule.
Ted [laughing]: Well, that's a relief.

The coach continued contextualizing by discussing with Ted how, when a necessary organizational task is not being done, others will tend to volunteer to do it, as these teachers were doing. In this way, she helped Ted see his teachers' bickering less as a personality issue, which he could do nothing about, and more as a system dynamic, which he could easily influence by formally taking up his role to do performance management of his teachers. By helping him make the connection between the system's goals, and his role in supporting those goals, the coach created the conditions for Ted to see the link between his failure to do performance management and his teachers' criticisms of each other. Ted responded readily, "I see now that the solution is for me to get over my reluctance to do performance management. I'd like to make that one of my goals for working with you as a coach."

Next, the coach worked with Ted to get clearer about where he was now in relation to this goal by doing a force-field analysis. Systems-centered coaching uses this exercise to help the client collect data about what is helping him move toward his goals (the "driving forces") and what is getting in his way (the "restraining forces"). Ted identified the driving and restraining forces for his goal of doing performance management of his teachers. He said that he had the skill, time, and knowledge to do performance management, but that he had trouble giving his teachers negative feedback.

With the coach's direction, Ted was then able to identify his restraining forces for giving negative feedback. He said that two of his teachers tend to argue with him at length, raising their voices at him. When this happens, he sees only two choices: either agree with them, in which case he isn't doing his job, or disagree with them, in which case they complain that he isn't listening and go on at him some more. He doesn't like either of these choices, so he simply drops the subject—until the next difficult incident arises.

The coach then took the next step in the force-field exercise, which is to help the client identify the restraining force that is easiest to reduce. It is often easier for a client to change his own behavior than it is for him to change other people's behavior. Therefore, the coach helped Ted clarify what was happening *inside him* that was getting in the way of responding effectively to these teachers.

Coach: When you realize that you want to give negative feedback to a teacher, what's the first thing that happens in you?

Ted: Well, let's say a parent calls me to complain about something a teacher has done, and I determine that what the teacher did was indeed a problem. Right away, I start to have this feeling of dread.
Coach: Do you have a thought at that point, that makes you feel dread?
Ted: Yes. My first thought, and I know this is silly, is "I'm going to lose my job."
Coach: Have you ever had this happen, that someone complained, and you lost your job?
Ted: No. I don't really believe I'm going to lose my job. It's just that on some level, I believe it's my job to fix the problem, and make everyone happy, and I know that I can't do that. I can't fix everyone's problems.
Coach: So when someone complains, you go into a mode where you believe it's your job to do the impossible?
Ted [laughs]: Yeah. I guess so. And I end up putting off dealing with it for two or three weeks, and the longer I put it off, the more distracted and stressed I get. I have a problem with anxiety. I did cognitive therapy for a while, but it didn't help as much as I had hoped. I know they are just anxious thoughts, but that doesn't stop them from happening.
Coach: In my experience, sometimes when we have anxious thoughts that distract us even though we don't believe them, it's because on some level we are using those anxious thoughts to distract us from something else going on that feels even more uncomfortable. For example, sometimes when we are angry or frustrated, but we don't feel like we can express it, we kind of suppress it, and feel anxious instead.
Ted: Well, that's me. I tend to suppress my frustration at work completely. Sometimes I take it out on my wife at home, which I shouldn't do. But there's really no one here who I can talk to about my frustration.
Coach: Do you feel any frustration right now?
Ted: Yes. I'm frustrated thinking about this situation.
Coach: Where in your body do you feel the frustration?
Ted: It's a tightness in my belly, and I feel kind of sick.

Systems-centered theory says that tightness and nausea are often signs of tension in our bodies that is literally constricting our "gut feelings," and preventing us from accessing the information contained in those feelings. The theory predicts that by releasing the tension, we will access the experience, and that by exploring the experience, we will gain insight into what we need to do to further the systems' goals. When the coach discussed this with Ted, he was able to take his frustration less personally and he expressed curiosity about what information his feelings might contain that might help the school function better. The coach then taught Ted how to release his tension and explore the experience it had been constricting. As he released his tension, Ted noticed that, at first, his anxiety went up. Systems-centered theory predicts that when we first try to undo tension, anxiety will come up and prevent us from fully undoing our tension. The coach discussed this with Ted and taught him how to undo his anxiety.

In the next session Ted reported that he had been practicing undoing tension and anxiety, and was feeling much less anxiety and more curiosity about the situation he was working on. The coach then introduced Ted to the systems-centered theory of maladaptive "roles." She reminded Ted of his earlier observation that he normally knows how to respond skillfully to complaints, but he sometimes goes into a mode in which he believes it's his job to "do the impossible," and becomes "de-skilled," and unable to access what he knows. She told Ted that systems-centered theory predicts that a person will regain access to their skills if they learn to catch themselves going into the "role" and choose not to go there. She then taught him some systems-centered techniques for catching the role when it comes up: (1) naming the role, (2) identifying the triggers for the role, and (3) noticing the "atmosphere" of the role (the thoughts, feelings, and beliefs that typically accompany it). Ted began by naming the role, "The Hero."

> Coach: What happens just before you get sucked into "Hero" mode?
> Ted: I have that sudden feeling of dread, and think "I'm going to lose my job."
> Coach: Do you see that your thought, "I'm going to lose my job," is a thought that something bad is going to happen in the future? What I was calling last time a "negative prediction"?
> Ted [surprised]: Yes, you're right. It is. So the dread is coming from my thought!
> Coach: Right.
> Ted: That's a tough one. I don't know if I could find my curiosity at that point.
> Coach: I think the first step is just to start noticing this thought when it happens, and recognizing that it is a trigger for you to go into your "Hero" mode. The earlier you can catch yourself being sucked into a mode, the easier it is to keep from being sucked in and staying there for two or three weeks. If you can catch yourself doing it, you may start to have more choices. To help you notice this triggering thought, and keep your balance with it, why don't you give your thought a pet name.
> Ted: Okay....let me think. Aha. It's the "Voice of Doom" thought.
> Coach: See if you can notice next time you have the Voice of Doom thought, label it, and notice what happens right after that. Then we can keep working on this and unpack it even more.

Follow-up session. Ted reported, with excitement and relief that he had gotten an email from a parent the previous week, complaining about a problem he knew he had to deal with. He noticed his characteristic feeling of dread, and realized right then that he had a choice: either get sucked into Hero mode by the Voice of Doom thought, and stew about it for two weeks, or take care of it right away. Immediately after this recognition, he felt a surge of energy, emailed the parent right away, and spoke calmly and directly about the problem that afternoon to the teacher involved.

Outcome. The coach continued coaching Ted for the rest of the academic year. He continued to be able to notice when he was getting sucked into "hero mode," and most of the time found he could now "take the bull by the horns" instead of putting off the task of giving negative feedback. He began developing a performance management process for his teachers. And he learned to access his anger and use the energy it gave him. In his words, "I had walled off my feelings, and now I am letting myself have feelings again. It feels absolutely wonderful!"

Case Example 5: Conflict Between Roles and Goals: A Middle Manager Learns to Create a Plan for Resolving a Conflict Between Himself and His Supervisor

Joyce works for Big Services Corporation where she leads the program development group for the eastern region. Recently, Big Services Corporation announced a reorganization that will bring together the group she leads and four other regional program development groups into a consolidated program development group. Joyce does not want to make any changes in the way she runs her group. The leader of the new Consolidated Program Development Group has scheduled weekly meetings with the leaders of the regional groups to create the new consolidated program development group. Joyce decides she will not attend. In her place, Joyce will send Sharon. Sharon reports to Joyce, functioning as the second-in-command for the eastern region program development group. One month after the announcement of the re-organization, Sharon and Joyce are in a conflict related to the reorganization. Sharon engages an SCT coach to help her plan a way to resolve the conflict.

> Sharon: I'm caught in a conflict with Joyce. We were in a meeting with the new Consolidated Program Development Group. I shared an idea that would require all of the regional groups to make a small change in how we market our products. After the meeting Joyce told me that she felt betrayed. She said it was clear that I had been working on the idea and hadn't shared it with her before the meeting. She asked, "What side are you on?" I feel terrible. I think I

have been sneaky. I knew Joyce did not want changes. I fear I am losing my integrity.
Coach: When you describe yourself as sneaky and say that you fear you have lost your integrity, you are making an interpretation. It sounds like you are attacking yourself. That won't help us develop an approach for resolving the conflict between yourself and Joyce.

Applying SCT Boundarying Methods

Boundarying methods help the client focus on information that is relevant for solving a problem. One step in boundarying is sorting facts from opinions and choosing to work with the facts first. In the dialogue above, the coach helps Sharon move away from an interpretation of her behavior so that she can focus on facts.

Sharon: I am not sharing my thoughts with Joyce about how we should work in relation to the reorganization.
Coach: What stands in the way of sharing your thoughts?
Sharon: I can see the situation from both sides, the needs of our regional group and the needs of the consolidated group. I am not sure where I weigh in. I waver. If I think about what is right for my career, I see it yet another way.
Coach: You have named three roles: an individual building a career, a member of a regional group and a member of the larger consolidated group. The wavering you describe appears to relate to different ways of seeing the reorganization from those roles. Let's look at your perspective on the re-organization from each if the three roles.

Applying SCT Contextualizing

SCT hierarchy defines three systems: the organization as a whole; the work unit; the member of the organization. Each system in the hierarchy provides a context for the next level of the hierarchy. SCT coaches help their clients discover how they can use their personal resources to achieve goals related to each context.

The coach working with Sharon suggested she start by describing the goals for each level of the organization. Sharon worked in this order: Big Services Corporation; Consolidated Program Development Group; Eastern Region Program Development Group, and her specific role as a leader of the Eastern Region Program Development Group; and finally, her role as an individual with career goals.

Once Sharon had identified the goals for each level, the coached used the SCT understanding of how to resolve conflicts. The coach guided Sharon through an exploration of similarities and differences between the goals at each level. This SCT method allows participants to discover similarities in perspectives that are apparently different and differences in perspectives that are apparently similar. For example, Sharon's coach asked her to explore how the reorganization was hindering the success of the Eastern Region Program Development Group (ERPDG) and how it supported the goals of the ERPDG. She engaged in the same exploration in relation to her personal career goals. Each aspect of Sharon's conflict was explored from one side and then the other. As Sharon explored, her role and her options at each level of the organization became clearer. When the exercise was complete, Sharon's experience of feeling sneaky had melted away. She had a developed a more complete understanding of the context and her preferences. She felt ready to approach Joyce to resolve the conflict.

> Coach: What have you learned that will help you resolve the conflict with Joyce?
> Sharon: It is easier for me to see both sides of the issue when I sort the information this way. I can see all four roles at once. I can see reasons for and against the reorganization in relation to our goals for our regional group. I want to share what I see and find out what she sees. I feel more confident that I can tell her what I see if I frame it as different perspectives seen from different roles. This makes it easier.
> Coach: Which of the four roles do you want to take to manage this meeting?
> Sharon: I will take my role as a member of the whole organization. This role has the other roles inside of it. I can see all of the roles from that position.

A week later, Sharon was relaxed and energetic as she described her meeting with Joyce. Sharon had been successful in sharing the information about roles. Joyce had readily shared information about what she saw from her different roles. They had explored similarities and differences in their perspectives. The most useful part of the conversation came when they both discovered that they felt the reorganization presented advantages and disadvantages. In addition, they found many areas of agreement; in fact, far more than Sharon would have predicted. Sharon felt great relief that their working relationship was restored. In addition, Sharon had learned SCT skills that she could use again. She learned how to see conflict in relation to roles and goals. She also learned to make a distinction between internal sources of conflict that arose between levels in her own hierarchy of roles and external conflict that arose between herself and others. She learned how to manage a meeting in which information from different roles could be shared and explored to make more effective decisions.

Conclusion

These six case examples provide a sampling of some of the ways systems-centered theory and techniques are being applied in an executive coaching context. The clients in the examples sought help for a range of reasons, from concern about job performance, to a loss of energy or motivation for work, to interpersonal conflicts. Regardless of the client's presenting complaint or particular goals, in every case, the coach was able to call on his or her knowledge of the theory of living human systems to choose precise and effective interventions. Because SCT assumes clients and organizations, like all living human systems, are innately goal-oriented, with an inherent drive towards survival, development, transformation, and environmental mastery (Agazarian, 1997), the coaches did not try to motivate their clients or teach them how to do their jobs better. Instead, the SCT coaches, using SCT theory, had only to elicit information from the client to determine where he or she was getting stuck and what internal obstacles were getting in his or her way, and then make the systems-centered intervention designed to reduce that particular restraining force. When clients were unclear about their roles or goals, the SCT coach helped them to explore what they knew about their roles and goals and to determine if they needed more information and how they would get it. If clients were trying to do work that was relevant to more than one context without discriminating between the different roles and goals that were appropriate to the different contexts, the SCT coaches began by helping them to clarify these and sort them out. If the clients were distracted by worries or distressed by physical tension or loss of energy, the coaches were able to use SCT protocols to release the energy bound up in these restraining forces so that it became available to the client for work. If the clients were caught in ineffective communication patterns, or information was not moving freely between them and others in the organizations, the coaches were able to use SCT protocols to help the client to shift to an effective communication pattern that improved information flow. Once they were freed from these defensive patterns and they and their colleagues had access to the information they needed from each other, these coaching clients became energized and grounded, and were able to find their own highly effective solutions to the work-related problems that were bothering them.

As coaches, we have found this approach satisfying, sensible, humane, and efficient. It is enormously helpful to have a unified, coherent, and robust theory that is applicable both to individuals and to organizations, and that explicitly makes the connection between the theory and the intervention. SCT shows us how to see our clients simultaneously as individual systems in themselves as well as voices speaking for a subgroup within their organizations, and how to make interventions that simultaneously help the individual and the organization. Understanding the theory, we can determine from the client's complaints *where* he or she is getting stuck, both personally and organizationally (i.e., in what phase of development). We can also identify *what* is getting in his or her way (i.e., what are the specific restraining forces we are observing). Since the theory predicts that in a given phase of development, certain tools will reduce certain obstacles, once we know the obstacles, we can draw on a toolbox of SCT techniques that are designed to work in that particular phase.

As these examples show, the result is that the clients' own existing knowledge and skills are freed up and directed effectively to support both their own professional goals and the goals of their organizations. They become clearer about their role, their goals, their organization's goals, and the lines of authority, accountability, and responsibility. Their communications become clearer and they learn how to get information they need from others more effectively. They develop more sense of choice. And they become energized for effective problem-solving.

3

Role, Goal and Context in an Organizational Intervention

Verena Murphy, LSW, Consultant

This chapter describes a case of using systems-centered theory to inform practice during an organizational intervention. It was possible to solve what initially appear to be problems entirely of a personal nature, by separating the Roles that the people in an organization hold from the personalities of the people. Furthermore, by separating the organizational Goals from the individual's Goals, and by considering all of them as part of the same context it was possible to view the same presenting issue from an objective point of view.

Systems-centered theory (Agazarian & Gantt, 2003) states that in the 'fight phase' of group development, 'scapegoating' individuals (Bion, 1961) is a commonly found phenomenon. This means that certain individuals become, or are seen as, "the problem" for the organization, while others are apparently free of any responsibility. The case described below illustrates the kind of scapegoating that occurs when individuals in an organization temporarily lose sight of their role, the organization's goal and the overall context in which everyone works.

This account is not intended as an example to follow of how to do an intervention. Rather, my aim is to describe how a systems-centered way of thinking about a problem influences what can be done about it. Second, I am not proposing this as an example to follow, because in hindsight I would do a few things differently. However, such an analysis would be the topic of a different chapter.

Theoretical Considerations

Agazarian (1997) defines an adaptive "role" as an "identifiable collection of behaviors that serve as driving forces toward the goal, appropriate to the context. It is a construct that is independent of the people who take on the role. One person changes their role many times a day: parent, spouse, employee, driver, guest, and so on. (p.xx). (we need the page number here for this quote" The important point here is that the role is separate from the person in the role, and in that way it is possible to separate an individual's personality (in SCT called "person system") from the way an individual performs the role. Thus, it increases the likelihood that an employee, who is given feedback, can see the feedback as being about the performance of the role, rather than a critique about his or her personality. This is especially useful because people often react to feedback with a vehement defense, as if their sense of self had just been attacked. Developing the skills not to take something "just personally" greatly influences a person's capacity to avoid being indiscriminately reactive. Instead the challenge is to remain centered and to view the feedback about the role performance and as an opportunity for learning how to use his or her resources for moving more effectively towards the goal (by identifying and weakening the restraining forces).

An important aspect of any role is the fact that each role requires authority[1] to implement the functions that come with the role, an awareness of the responsibility (appropriate behavior) that goes along with the role, and accountability to the next higher level in the system. To perform effectively in a role, all three—Authority, Responsibility and Accountability—are necessary.

Approach

The title of this chapter suggests a progressive description of role, goal and context. However, I will describe the set of circumstances, as they became apparent to me during the interviews I conducted at the beginning of this consultation. The account therefore presents the information as I received it. The initial goal of developing a working climate among opposing parties, combined with a plan for implementing "next steps" was met in the one-day intervention.

As I am describing the case, I am including the thoughts I had at the time the information became available. They are written in *italics.*

Referral for the Consultation

The referral came from an instructor at a mid-western educational institution, who felt that a systems-orientation would be the most useful given the circumstances of 'the organization in trouble,' which I will call Multiplex [2]. She had heard about the situation at Multiplex from "Sherrie," the supervisor of the orga-

---

1. Authority, Responsibility and Accountability are discussed later in the chapter.
2. Multiplex is a pseudonym intended to protect the confidentiality of the organization.

nization. Sherrie told her that she had been approached by her superior, the vice president of the educational institution. He had asked Sherrie to "do something about the situation at Multiplex" as the organization's office staff had approached him directly about the state of affairs and told him they felt that Sherrie's prior attempts at resolving the issues had not resulted in their desired changes. At this point I still did not know what was meant by "the situation." As I spoke with Sherrie, I discovered the facts as she understood them.

Multiplex was founded by Dan, who responded to a desire by many students at the educational institution to gain experience in the "real world" through volunteer positions in the community. His role initially was to procure the locations and positions in the community and also to serve as a student liaison. As the demand for such volunteer positions grew, the demand also rose for paid office staff, and finding financial support for those paid positions became an additional task for the director. In the first few years, Dan had been able to meet the goal by routinely working overtime. In recent months, his priority had changed to devoting more time to a new set of personal obligations, and the dramatic shift in work hours and his presence in the office resulted in the conflict presented below.

The Context as Described by the Supervisor and the Staff of Multiplex

Upon meeting with the supervisor, Sherrie, I wanted to find out about the organization and its systems hierarchy as well as the formal organizational hierarchy. SCT theory defines a hierarchy of isomorphic systems which are similar in structure and function (Agazarian & Gantt, 2000). Identifying the systems hierarchy would give me a picture of the context for each subsystem. Each subsystem in a systems hierarchy exists in the context of a system above it and is the context for a subsystem.

Talking to Sherrie, I was able to find out that Multiplex existed in the context of the educational institution, and that Multiplex was itself the context for Dan's role and the roles of the administrative staff. By identifying the larger system context, I could then identify the educational institution as the larger context that affects every hierarchical level below it. Using SCT thinking, what we know about one level in the system can inform us about another level. For example, if the larger context abides by strict rules and regulations, these will affect the way the departments below are operating.

In this case the educational institution was a place of much academic freedom, where individuals were rather free in how they managed their roles, as long as they fulfilled the institution's goal, which was to maximize their students' education.

I also asked about the formal hierarchy of the organization. Who reported to whom? The organization's hierarchy was reported to be the following:

Figure 1   The Organization's Hierarchy

President of the Educational Institution and a Government Agency
Vice President of the Educational Institution
Program Supervisor "Sherrie"
Program Director "Dan"
Office staff
Volunteers

I was informed that Multiplex's staff had provided Sherrie with a list of complaints. They apparently had been feeling overwhelmed for many months and their primary target was Dan's behavior.

Multiplex was started by Dan, who had devoted up to 60 hours per week for several years in order to make it a viable and growing enterprise. He wanted to serve the student community at the institution by creating "real world" experiences and learning opportunities outside the classroom for them. In return, the students received community service credits for their work. He worked on establishing the community liaisons and relationships that he hoped would result in more opportunities for students.

A toned-down version of a few of the staff's angry sounding complaints on the list they submitted to Sherrie were as follows:

Dan is not listening to his staff. *(This, I re-framed to myself as a lack of information transfer from one system to another, as Dan's role is a system).*

Dan cut down his actual work hours to half of a 40-hour week. *(This got me curious. There must be a valid reason for this shift in energy that he now directed towards the job. The question then arose whether that shift made it possible for Dan to nevertheless fulfill his job responsibilities. Along with Authority comes Responsibility and Accountability. To what extent were these exercised? The staff's feelings were that he was not fulfilling his role responsibilities. Sherrie was not sure about that, because she had no evidence to the contrary from her perspective. Therefore this question needed further clarification).*

Dan does not show up for work when he is expected, and the staff can't locate him. The staff feels they often have to cover for his frequent absences and invent excuses, because they don't know where he is or when he will be back in the office. *(This complaint indicated the presence of ambiguity in the system that would need clarification).*

Dan refuses to do day-to-day duties required of a Program Director, just because he thinks he is "above it." Therefore, it's always up to staff to pick up the slack. We have already enough to do. *(I noticed the anger and frustration particularly in this complaint and the possible need at some point during the consult for the staff to explore their feelings through the SCT method of "functional subgrouping").*

Dan is making decisions that directly affect the staff without informing them, much less exploring with them how his decision will affect their workload. This often results in the staff having to work overtime or let prior commitments slide in order to meet the new obligations. *(This data suggested to me that Dan was acting on his freedom to use his authority as he saw fit without consulting anyone, which was congruent with the norm of the entire educational institution, where the largest body—the educators—were rather free in how they managed their day-to-day operations. There were, of course, driving and restraining forces associated with that fact, which could be explored during the consult, if the energy for such an exploration was there. The fact that staff had more work as a result of these independent actions, suggested to me that Dan's lack of collecting information from his staff was a restraining force in the organization (a restraining force towards the goal of efficient use of resources in the system).*

At the same time, Dan's action—deliberately not collecting information from his subordinates—seemed to be isomorphic (similar in structure and function) to what happened at the system levels above. For example, according to Sherrie's account, the relatively rare meetings she had with the vice president—himself a very busy man—indicated that he was not in the habit of collecting information about Multiplex from her either.

The complaints were of a more personal nature and related to the "lack of order" in Dan's office, or his unpredictable "mood swings," or his "lack of respect for his all-female employees."

In the recent past the staff had contacted the vice president of Multiplex, since, in their opinion, Sherrie had not been able to provide the desired influence on Dan to remedy the situation. Given the list of complaints formulated by the staff, and the vice president's then delegating "the problem" back to Sherrie, she felt herself drawn into the possibility of having to confront Dan. To prevent a potential fight, she sought the help of a consultant.

Sherrie asked me whether or not she should confront Dan and use the list as evidence against him. I asked her whether her goal was to create a fight, because the language used in the list of complaints contained many SAVI[3] Red Light behaviors—outright "attacks," which would likely invite a "defense" response, and therefore encourage a fight. Sherrie's goal was just the opposite. She decided not to confront Dan with the list, and I kept the staff's information, including their enormous sense of frustration and exhaustion in the back of my mind.

Assessment for the Intervention

Ideally, I would have liked to work with the members at all levels of the hierarchy, particularly with the staff, to frame their feelings of frustration as a normal reaction when a pattern of behavior is not in sync with the changing demands of the organization. After subgrouping work around their feelings, I would have prepared them to approach Dan in such a way that he could hear the staff's concerns and not take them just personally. When a group can reframe their complaints (into proposals) it is easier for the authority in charge to hear all the information in the group, whatever the content. Had I had enough time to work with this system I would have helped the staff reframe the complaints as proposals: (which is a SAVI technique). For example: Complaint: "You never let us know when you will be in the office!"—Proposal: "Let us know when you expect to be back. It would be helpful to our clients if we could tell them the time of day you plan to be back at the office."

In addition, given more time, I would have worked with Dan to understand that his company was moving into the authority issue phase and, therefore, his employees' complaints about his change in his work structure were not only appropriate for the phase of development but, in fact, predictable. The phase of development is "fight" (Bennis & Shepard, 1956; Agazarian, 1981, 1994, 1999; Agazarian & Gantt, 2003). When employees can confront their bosses with their frustrations, and the boss can see the employees' frustration as a useful next step in the system's development, it shifts the energy from targeting the supervisor (the authority), and is instead used for joint problem solving within the agency (Trey, 2002).

The above-mentioned intervention and learning process, however takes more time than the organization was prepared to invest. I had at most one day for the consultation, which influenced the type of intervention I was able to do. Instead of preparing Dan for a confrontation by his employees, I decided to reduce the staff's authority issue by placing their roles and goals into the larger context in which they were all working.

---

3. SAVI is a System for Analyzing Verbal Interaction that helps identify verbal patterns that facilitate either a climate of communication that is intimate (through the use of "green light verbal behaviors"), neutral ("yellow light verbal behaviors"), or likely to invite a fight ("red light verbal behaviors") Simon & Agazarian, (1967).

Sherrie and I agreed that she and Dan would participate in the one-day consultation, and that I would meet with Dan separately beforehand, because I had not yet received his understanding of the situation. I was also anticipating that Dan might experience some anxiety because this intervention was imposed on him, and, therefore, I wanted to explore his concerns and expectations about the consult separately, where the chance of public exposure was minimized.

It is important here to appreciate the necessity that all information be in the system, that is why (for lack of available other participants in the hierarchy, e.g., the vice president and the president) I asked Sherrie and Dan to be a part of the work group, so they could hear what the concerns were and to participate by contributing to the system whatever information they thought was appropriate. Therefore, my reason for including Sherrie in the all day intervention was that I wanted her to have the full information of what transpired that day. She then could make appropriate recommendations to her supervisor, the vice president of the educational institution who, with the president's support was in a position to make decisions about implementation.

The Context as Described by Dan, the Program Director of Multiplex

As mentioned above, this not-for-profit organization was partially funded by, and under the guidance of, both a mid-western educational institution and a government funded agency, whose funding was, however, unpredictable. The educational institution gave Dan a lot of autonomy in how he ran Multiplex. The government agency, however, required much documentation and accountability of the way their funds were spent.

Dan had over the years worked very hard to develop not just the organizational structure, but also its outreach to the community. Over the prior year his personal circumstances had changed so significantly that he felt a need to shift his priorities. In fact, he stated that he did reduce his work hours to about 30 hours of the standard 40-hour a week position. *(As, prior to his private commitments, he had worked 60 hours per week just to keep up, he in fact reduced his work hours to half that amount. No wonder the staff felt exhausted—apparently the responsibility fell on them to provide the same services that Dan's prior diligence helped provided.)* According to Dan, most of his current 30 hours were spent on applying for grants to secure funding for his staff. His goal was to make sure his employees had a job. What he saw as his strengths, however, was his role as liaison to the community, and less so his grant writing.

Given the success of Multiplex on the one hand and the unpredictable financial support on the other, the pressure on Dan to secure additional funds increased. However, based on years of successful experience, he felt he could trust his staff to manage the office, while he pursued creative ways to keep the organization afloat. He hoped that making new contacts in the community would lead to more service or funding opportunities. Besides, according to Dan "it should not be his job to shuffle paperwork that could be handled by anyone." He saw Sherrie as a friend with whom he could consult as needed, and, according to him, she had been supportive of his endeavors in the past.

This leaves open the possibility that he either conveyed to her only information that he knew she would likely approve of, or that Sherrie found it difficult to disagree with Dan. Either way, it was not up to me to speculate about the personal dynamics between the two, but to remain clear on whether the goals of their roles and the institution's goals were being met.

Explicit and Implicit Roles and Goals

The following sections include descriptions of the goals and roles of each of the parties in the organizational hierarchy. By "explicit" we mean the stated or intended role or goals that that can be verified by written documents or verbal statements individuals made about them. Often, explicit roles or goals differ from what actually happens in the real world. The goal that can be inferred from what really happens is called "the implicit" role or goal. The discrepancy between the explicit and implicit impacts the organizational functioning. The stated driving forces in an organization or a team will relate to its explicit roles and goals. When we identify the restraining forces (those actions that are in the way of the goals) we can discern the "implicit" roles and goals that compete with the explicit, as will be evident in the section below describing "The Intervention".

The Educational Institution's Goal (The Goal of the Context)

From my conversations with Sherrie and Dan, I learned that one of the explicit goals of the educational institution was to further the efforts of the organization through partial funding for the program. Based on prior occasions where the vice president had been approached and the apparent lack of interest in the details of Multiplex, the institution's implicit goal was largely to refrain from interfering with the organization's day-to-day operations and to leave the supervision in the hands of Sherrie.

The educational institution's role. Its role is to create an environment where creative ideas can be expressed, explored, and put into practice, and to support those individuals who have the energy, time and resources for implementing endeavors that support the institution's goal.

The Supervisor's Goal

Sherrie's explicit goal was to help support Dan in his endeavors while not letting it interfere with the demands of her other full-time occupation and to serve as liaison to the educational institution's leadership. Based on her account of actual time spent consulting to Dan, it was evident that her implicit goal was to provide that support in the role of a confidante and to interfere as little as possible in his affairs, because over the years she had come to trust Dan to know what was best for the organization. This data was confirmed by Dan during my fact finding sessions with him.

The supervisor's role. Sherrie saw her explicit role as only marginally involving her, as Dan had developed Multiplex almost single handedly in the previous ten years. Therefore she considered it "his project." Her reliance on his authority and experience made possible her implicit role as a supportive friend.

The Program Director's Goal

Dan's explicit goal was to further develop Multiplex by seeking new and creative ways to increase funding for the employees' salaries and to broaden services to the clients. This goal was supported by his staff. Based on his own account and that of his office staff, his implicit goal was to achieve this development with as little time spent at the office as possible, and most of it spent as liaison to the community, in the service of long-range planning.

The program director's role. Dan saw his explicit leadership role at Multiplex as one of making sure that the organization developed, which meant he had to secure funding at all cost. While serving as a community liaison, he was intent on finding new financial resources and new ways of serving the community.

His implicit role was one of not getting involved with staff's programming concerns, as he trusted their competence of being able to manage the office without him just fine.

The Staff's Goal

The explicit goal of the office staff was to deliver the services that Multiplex advertised and to do so in a reliable and efficient manner. Based on their account of what actually occurred (the lack of Dan's presence in the office), the staff's implicit goal became to increase the director's presence in his office, and to have him include their input before making decisions that directly affected them. *Note: the staff's goal differed from the director's goal, whose goal had been to find ways to secure the funding for their jobs.* This difference was at the heart of the conflict.

The staff's role. The staff's explicit role was that of managing the day-to-day operations of Multiplex within the role responsibilities made explicit in their job descriptions. The staff's implicit role was to take up the program director's role when he was absent.

Considerations Regarding Roles

Human beings step in and out of roles all the time, whether we are conscious of the shifts or not (Agazarian & Gantt, 2000). Whether we are in the role of son/daughter, parent, partner, driver, guest, lover of pets, visitor, student, teacher, cook, friend, or in any professional role, the important part to remember is that every role has its own goal. In a professional hierarchy, such as an institution, the role of dean of a particular college is different from the role of an instructor, in that the dean may be accountable to different board members and responsible for the performance of an entire college, whereas the role of the instructor is to be accountable to the dean of the college and responsible for the students to meet their learning objectives. The authority (power, influence) that the position of dean carries is also different from the authority the role of instructor contains, and again different from the authority administrative support staff carries. At best, authority, responsibility and accountability are all present in a role, but at times it is possible that an employee has all of the responsibility of a job and accountability to a superior, but has not been given the authority that the role entails, which often results in a frustrated employee. As an organizational consultant, it is useful to ascertain what the employees' status of authority, responsibilities and accountability is before making any intervention. This includes collecting data about the difference between explicitly stated authority (what is written in a contract) and the implicit authority (what actually happens on the job—e.g., does the authority actually lie with a superior and not the employee).

Assessment Summary

As is evident from the staff's list of complaints in this case, their program director served as a scapegoat for the whole organization. However, the staff directed much less frustration at the supervisor, and even less at the vice president of the organization, even though the responsibility for how an organization functions lies at every system level, particularly at the top level in the hierarchy, which has the ultimate accountability.

What is also evident are the similarities (which relates to SCT's understanding of isomorphy) found at every system level, e.g., a tendency to take a "hands off" approach which borders on blind trust as valuable information was either not available, avoided or not considered.

From looking at the list of the staff's complaints, the most important one appeared to be the dramatic reduction in the hours Dan spent at the office, and most other complaints were about the consequences of that reduction, which generated feelings of frustration, anger, and resentment.

The goal of the intervention was to clarify roles, the authority that comes with the role, the responsibilities inherent in the role and to clarify accountability. This could be done by keeping in mind the goals of Multiplex and the context in which it operated. An important feature of the intervention was to change Dan's implicit role as a scapegoat.

The Intervention

Sherrie and I decided on a one-day retreat (9am–5pm) for the entire staff, including Dan and Sherrie, with a lunch provided at noon. Ideally, I wanted to work with everyone in the room at the same time, so the information that surfaced was available to all concerned.

Dan's stated preference the day before had been that the staff would meet with me alone at first and that he would remain available nearby and join the staff when it was useful. Independently, this idea was very much supported by the staff. They were adamant that they did not wish to be in the same room with Dan. They felt that whatever facts or feelings they conveyed would be downplayed or made irrelevant by Dan. They reportedly could not match his well-developed oratory skills, especially his tendency to diverge from issues they felt were important to issues he considered more urgent. They had not succeeded in being heard in the past and they were not hopeful it was going to happen this time.

While respecting their wish, I placed their concern in the larger context of an institution that was based on giving instructors autonomy and academic freedom; therefore it could be expected that certain individuals working within such an environment would make use of this "freedom" to the fullest extent, perhaps even pushing the boundaries—and by doing so perhaps inadvertently asking that the boundaries be more clearly defined. The staff, of course, was focused on the harsh consequences his "freedom to act" had had for them.

Therefore, I first explored with the staff their feelings, which centered on not being heard and their typical response to not feeling heard. I did this by using the SCT method of "functional subgrouping," (Agazarian, 1997) a method for integrating differences. This is done by having those members speak together who share similar feelings and experiences and then making space for those members who feel differently to talk together. In our meeting, the integration of all the voices resulted in frustration and anger being expressed, including a sense of exasperation and physical exhaustion due to increased work for them. This combined with a sense of futility and helplessness and a readiness to quit their jobs. They all stated that if they had alternate positions elsewhere and/or if they hadn't felt such commitment to the work, they would no longer be at Multiplex. They also expressed appreciation for having an opportunity to explore and express their feelings, as well as finding joint support without having to fear retaliation.

When I asked Sherrie about her experience, she shared some of the staff's sense of frustration and helplessness. Two hours into our work, even I experienced some frustration, because I had realized that the staff was still not ready to have Dan join our work in progress! Remembering the importance of keeping an eye on "role, goal and context," I decided to take the issue that had very much been personalized up until then, and develop a goal in the hope everyone could support it.

Jointly, the staff verbalized an attainable and realistic goal they would have liked to see the organization achieve: to create a working environment, including a supportive emotional climate that promotes the reliable delivery of services to the clients.

We then generated a list of driving forces towards that goal. I first helped the staff reframe their complaints as proposals. For example, "Dan is not listening to his staff" became "Collect data from staff and use the information for joint problem solving." The complaint: "Dan cut down his work hours to half of a 40-hour week" became the proposal: "The program director will evaluate with the supervisor whether the present work hours are adequate to fulfill the position's role responsibilities." Complaint: "Dan does not show up for work when he is expected, and the staff can't locate him. The staff feels they often have to cover for his frequent absences and invent excuses, because they don't know where he is, or when he will be back in the office." Proposal: "In order for the office responsibilities to be carried out in a timely and predictable manner, the program director will inform the staff when he will not be in the office."

At this point the staff had not yet moved from using the director as a scapegoat, but I was guiding the group towards collecting facts and data about the work, which made the issue not about "the people" but about the combined "task." At that point I asked the staff whether it was a good time to call the director into the meeting to see whether their goal for the organization was the same goal that Dan was working towards. The staff agreed to have Dan join the meeting in progress because they could see that it was functional to have all the voices of the group working on a common task.

Having the staff's goal clearly spelled out helped Dan orient right away to the work that had been done so far. He was, in fact, surprised that the stated goal was not something that had been already achieved, but was something the staff still wanted to work towards. The discussion that ensued between the staff and Dan elucidated their different views about the state of the office. Dan seemed very surprised by the staff's sense of frustration and defended himself at first by stating how his primary goal and concern was for staff to have a paid job. He very eloquently defended his previous actions as all related to his efforts towards keeping the staff employed. It almost sounded like none of the staff's grievances were justified because of this all-encompassing reason that the staff apparently did not appreciate enough.

As mentioned above, during this intervention there was a strong pull into blaming and defending—in short personalizing the actions that had preceded this meeting. Therefore, I wanted to stay with data, rather than opinion (an important SCT strategy for building a problem-solving culture), so I asked Dan, whether the staff's stated goal written on the board was a goal he could support, or if there was anything he would like to add or change. After reviewing the stated goal, he was in support of it as the staff had formulated it.

To reduce again the tendency towards blaming, I placed the stated goal in the context of the reality that the organization had over the years developed from a relatively simple service provider to a much more complex one. A review of whether or not the current structure was adequate could be a useful undertaking for all of them.

Relating to the stated goal and keeping in mind the larger context, I encouraged everyone to collect data and facts, rather than opinions, about what behaviors had moved the group toward the goal in the past, and what behaviors they could identify that had moved them away from the goal. We created the force field described below [SCT (Agazarian, 1986; Agazarian & Gantt, 2000) has adapted Lewin's (1951) force field.]—a method for identifying the driving and restraining forces towards a goal—and spent the remainder of the day reorienting from 'attack, blame and defend' dialogue to collecting facts and data.

The force field example below served to keep the conversation oriented to the work goals and at the same time it was a list of concrete guidelines of driving forces (what one would want to do more of) and restraining forces (what one would want to do less of).

Figure 2   FORCE FIELD

Goal: To create a working environment, including a supportive emotional climate, that promotes the reliable delivery of services to clients.

Driving Forces towards the goal +	Restraining Forces towards the goal −
- Consider staff's feedback in decision making and problem solving process - Developing a procedure for following up on and actions - Collecting information - Having supervisor present at staff meetings	- Making assumptions - Contradictions between intentions and actions - Items identified as "next steps" - Ambiguity about work schedules - Not using available information - Making negative predictions

Outcome

By staying with the common goal, but most importantly by seeing the context that the organization today was more complex than even five years ago, Dan was able to question whether the time he could realistically devote towards his job role responsibilities was sufficient. He wondered out loud whether it would be a good idea to consult human resources about the possibility of shifting his work hours to a number that was congruent with his private obligations. This included exploring the possibility of separating his full time job into two part-time jobs, or adding a new position altogether.

The staff seemed to derive some satisfaction from hearing Dan owning some responsibility in the shift that was affecting his staff's working condition.

Sherrie, in turn, could see that her attending staff meetings would serve a functional role for the staff. She would not have to rely on hearsay either from staff or from Dan, but had direct access to how decisions were arrived at and could ensure accountability from everyone. However, she was left with the question, how, in reality, she would be able to participate more often in her supervisory capacity without neglecting her other full time duties. It became apparent that exploring that question required more time than had been made available for the consult.

By focusing on role, goal and context, the intervention made a dialogue possible that otherwise might have left emotional scars from a potentially harsh verbal confrontation. Alternately, the organization might have been left in the same place because pertinent information never surfaced for fear of retaliation. Instead, while everyone felt very tired by the end of the day, they also were satisfied that some difficult issues had been addressed in a collegial climate with "next steps" in place awaiting implementation.

A few months later, Sherrie reported that she has been attending the staff meetings, taking notes and following the progress of agenda items. According to her, the staff has followed her example of voicing their differences in the staff meetings and, as a result, there have been some improvements in accountability on everyone's part. Since the program will soon be required to collaborate with another newly-designed program that the educational institution launched two years earlier, a shift in the hierarchical structure will likely result. Dan will likely be able to concentrate on what he loves to do: to be the community liaison, and the "procurer of funds." The job of seeking funding will likely go to someone whose passion is in writing grants. Two staff members left during the summer months to seek other positions, but those who had been at Multiplex the longest, still remain.

Summary

In this chapter I have described an organizational intervention that was ostensibly about a program director's lack of accountability and the resulting mounting frustration to his office staff.

When approaching "the presenting problem" from a systems-centered perspective, however, it is possible to diffuse a potentially hostile and confrontational situation (or one that is locked in silent frustration) into a productive dialogue by simply focusing on the parties' roles and goal clarifications and a reminder of their given larger context.

The human tendency to personalize differences (e.g., targeting individuals who deviate from a norm or from certain expectations) is thereby prevented, and the system focuses on the structure that defines the boundaries of each role within the system. A broader understanding is then gained of the driving and restraining forces of role performance instead of on the personalities of those within these roles.

4

From Complaints to Strategies: Using an Agency's All-Staff Meetings as a Learning Lab for Understanding System Dynamics

Dorothy Gibbons, LCSW, Consultant

This chapter describes the results of a 10-month experiment in functional subgrouping by the staff of one department in a social service agency during that agency's monthly all-staff meetings. This experiment was initially designed to decrease the staff's frustration during these meetings. However, the surprising discovery was that instead of decreasing their frustration, functional subgrouping made the staff *more* aware of their frustration and the restraining forces they had been using to avoid their awareness of it. With the subgroup system serving as a container for their frustration, staff became more energized and curious about the system dynamics that were being enacted in these meetings. As the staff gained a new level of understanding of system dynamics, they developed more effective strategies for participating in all-staff meetings and for negotiating the agency's bureaucratic system. However, even more important, they used their knowledge of system dynamics to create better therapeutic systems as they worked with their clients, families, and groups.

"Location, Location, Location." With these words, I used to remind the clinical staff of my department how important it was to pay attention to the context whenever they became frustrated with their clients or with the some of the bureaucratic decisions in the small social service agency in which we worked. Our department was the Juvenile Sex Offender (JSO) department, so of course our clients had issues with power and authority. Our agency was used to generous city funding, so of course it was stressful when our city contracts were replaced with the much-less-lucrative managed care reimbursements. Building on the SCT understandings about context, I would tell the staff that if they kept the realities of the context in mind, they would be much less likely to get frustrated each time they encountered an obstacle to their goals. Although, as a department, we were able to incorporate this SCT understanding into our clinical work, we had much more difficulty keeping the realities of our workplace in mind. It was not until we consciously decided to use what we knew about SCT to manage the frustrations of working in the agency that we came to a true understanding of the importance of locating ourselves squarely in the reality of the workplace.

This chapter describes a10-month experiment using functional subgrouping in the agency's all-staff meetings. As a result of this experiment, the clinical staff freed up its energy, moved out of a helpless, complaining position and became proactive problem solvers. As employees, they learned to be adept at negotiating the bureaucratic system, and they learned about systems first-hand.

As the director of a Juvenile Sex Offender department in a not-for-profit agency that treated both victims and offenders of sexual abuse, I constantly stressed the importance of working from a systems perspective. I emphasized the importance of paying attention to the layers of systems—the clients' families, neighborhoods, schools, justice system, and general culture—that helped to shape the clients' beliefs and behaviors. Our clients' lives were nested inside these systems and, therefore, greatly affected by their values and norms. Systems-centered theory refers to these layers of systems as a "hierarchy" of systems, and postulates that all systems in the hierarchy are "isomorphic," or similar in structure and function (Agazarian, 1997). According to systems-centered theory, who we are at any particular moment has more to do with the system we are in than our individual characteristics. Given this understanding of system dynamics, I stressed that once our clients entered treatment, our department became part of the hierarchy of isomorphic systems that affected their lives, so the norms that we set as a department affected the work that we did with our clients. With this isomorphy in mind, we monitored the communication patterns in our meetings, we subgrouped around differences, and we paid attention to our impulses to scapegoat or create identified patients in our work with each other as well as with our work with the clients.

When I was hired as director in 1998 (I was the fourth director of the JSO department in 3 years), the department faced serious problems: high turnover of clinicians, poor client attendance, and a low rate of compliance with treatment. Treatment plans were seriously out-of-date and progress notes were months behind. Also, there was an atmosphere of barely suppressed hostility as clinicians engaged in power struggles with both clients and the previous department director who now had another position in the agency. As isomorphy would suggest, these problems existed in the agency-as-a-whole as well as in the JSO department. In my first year, the agency experienced an 86% change over in staff; during my first 18 months, the agency had 3 CEO's; after an agency-wide chart audit by the city, we were described as "an agency in chaos"; and there was a general atmosphere of contention and discontent throughout the agency.

Creating a Boundary

When I first arrived as the new JSO director and saw the chaos in the entire organization, I decided to "circle the wagons' and to concentrate on building a clinically sound, revenue-producing department. I was successful in doing this by creating a firm boundary between the JSO department and the rest of the agency. I purposely kept many of the limitations and the frustrations of the larger agency out of my department's awareness—often by taking on administrative tasks far beyond my designated role. I worked to shore up problems in the Medical Records and Intake as problems in these departments directly affected my department. I encouraged clinicians to come to me with administrative difficulties so that I could mediate with the support staff or agency administrators, and I kept much of the "informal" information about changes in the agency out of the department until such changes became official.

By keeping this strict boundary, I was able to create a cohesive clinical team by emphasizing the clinicians' role as therapists in the JSO department and de-emphasizing their roles as employees in the larger agency. For several years, this "circling of the wagons" was very helpful for the development of the JSO department. We were isolationists, and as far as our clinical work was concerned, this approach was functional. During my five-year tenure as Director, the JSO department had the highest rate of staff retention in the agency, the highest compliance scores for documentation in the managed care audits (95%), and the highest ratings in the entire city for efficacy of treatment of juvenile sex offenders. We also had the highest client-show rate, and, as a result, the JSO department was the only revenue-producing department in the agency.

Because of my systems-centered training, I knew that this success could not last—sooner or later the problems in the larger context would begin to affect our department. The inevitability of "isomorphy" haunted me, and I knew that it was only a matter of time before our department would either lose its momentum and succumb to the lower performance norms of the larger agency, or that the many administrative problems in the larger agency would begin to frustrate the clinicians and affect their performance. However, I continued to keep a relatively closed boundary between the department and management, vectoring the therapists' attention towards the clinical work. During my fifth year as Director, keeping this boundary relatively impermeable became more and more difficult. A "culture of blame" was developing in the agency; the CEO made statements at meetings about the low functioning of all of the clinicians, despite data to the contrary about particular clinicians who had consistently exceeded the utilization standard. Clinicians, in turn, started scrutinizing the performance of workers throughout the agency—in both clinical and billing departments—in order to divert the blame from themselves. Gradually, over the course of about a year, I watched the JSO clinicians become more and more involved with the "high drama" of the agency: engaging in negative gossip in the hallways, constantly complaining about their working conditions, making sarcastic remarks about management, and behaving as if they were helpless. I noticed that they were becoming more and more frustrated with me for not protecting them from the agency's problems. I also noticed how all this attention to the overall agency was draining our energy from the clinical work we all valued.

As director, I also felt helpless and frustrated. I had more information than the clinical staff did about the workings of the agency, and I had serious concerns about many of the management decisions. However, I had no way then of bringing in my frustration without leaving my leadership role and joining the complaining and gossiping which as a systems-centered practitioner I knew would weaken my role and contribute to "noise" in the system. I became aware that by holding a firm boundary between my department and the larger agency, I had created a rich environment for the clinical work, but I had limited the staff's awareness of the agency context in which they worked as employees. Also, I had inadvertently created a culture of dependency on me as an idealized leader, and I was now experiencing the costs of the culture I had fostered.

The more the staff complained, the more frustrated I became with their unrealistic expectations of the organization. I found myself wishing that there were some way that they could experience, first-hand, the frustrations that I usually experienced when working with the agency's management team. The solution came when I recognized that at all-staff meetings, I was on the same level or in the same subsystem as my clinical staff. We were all in the employee subsystem, and in the context of these meetings, we often experienced the same frustration and sense of helplessness as I did in my director role. The difference was that in these meetings I did not have the same role responsibilities to hold a boundary. We all had access to the same information and experience in these meetings. In all-staff meetings, there was a management and an employee subsystem, with the management system being very active and the employee system being passive.

As I thought this through from my SCT perspective, I realized that what was missing from the all-staff meetings was an intermediate subsystem in which we could all come together with our shared goals for the agency, despite our particular roles in the agency hierarchy. We needed a way to join each other with our work energy so we could link all of our resources for achieving our common goals for the agency and for the clients we served. In other words, we needed what SCT calls a subgroup system (Agazarian, 1997) to tap and direct the energy of the agency as we worked towards our common goals. With this in mind, I encouraged the JSO department to engage in an experiment to create a subgrouping system in the all-staff meetings.

Getting Started

As I sat in the all-staff meetings, I knew something was missing. The meetings all *looked* like meetings: we had agendas, reports, and once in a while a decision, but it felt like dead space. The agency staff was lifeless and unresponsive. Even the members of the JSO department, so full of energy, ideas and good humor, in our department meetings, sat in silence with downcast eyes throughout these monthly mandatory all-staff meetings. When I attempted to subgroup and join lone voices in these meetings, my attempts fell flat and were usually followed by an awkward silence, until we moved on to the next item on the agenda.

I approached this issue with my staff at a department meeting. I told them how I had noticed their pattern of silence at the all-staff meetings, and I described my own frustration at these meetings. I mentioned how I noticed that although clinicians habitually subgrouped in department meetings, they did not use these skills in the all-staff meetings. I asked if anyone else was with me in feeling frustrated during these meetings. After a period of silence, the staff began to talk about how they were more aware of feeling helplessness rather than frustration. They reported that they "go numb" and "zone out." One member described the meetings as having the flatness of "an in-person email" and another stated that as she picked up the sandwich that the agency provided at these meetings, she felt like she was accepting her "last meal before being bored to death."

Identifying the Restraining Forces

As the staff explored their flatness, the energy began to rise. As I had previously introduced the systems-centered focus on identifying and weakening restraining forces to the staff, it was relatively easy for us to shift into exploring the restraining forces to their subgrouping in the all-staff meetings. Staff members stated that because most comments were either ignored or met with "yes-buts" in the meetings, they had learned to keep a low profile and not call attention to themselves. They had negative predictions that if they did speak up or if they joined a lone voice, they would be left out on a limb. Finally, they said that there seemed to be an implicit message that our role as employees was to listen silently and not hold up the agenda with comments and questions. The staff felt that there was a pressure in the room to get through the agenda quickly and end the meeting early.

Several things became clear. First, there was no explicit goal to subgroup. Whereas in the JSO meetings we had committed ourselves to functional subgrouping in order to create an environment that managed conflict so that we, as a department, could be a containing environment for the clinical work, there was no clear commitment to subgroup with the larger agency. Second, a functional subgrouping system doesn't just happen; it has to be consciously built. Without having an explicit functional subgrouping system in place, any employee who decided to join or build in the all-staff meeting was doing so on his or her own, without support.

And so, as a department, we intentionally subgrouped around the driving and restraining forces for creating a subgroup system in all-staff meetings. The major restraining force was a sense of futility—why bother subgrouping in a meeting where the administrators don't want to hear our ideas anyway? As we got clearer that convincing the administration that our ideas were right was not actually the goal of functional subgrouping, the staff identified functional subgrouping as a way to create an atmosphere in which energy and ideas had a chance to percolate. With this understanding, the department became more curious about the possibility of experimenting with functional subgrouping within the larger agency context. For driving forces, we recognized we could test our SCT hypotheses that a positive change in all-staff meetings would have a positive effect on our department as well as on the therapist-client systems below us; we could build a climate in which new ideas would have a chance to "breathe"; we could be part of a subgroup "team" in the meeting and could rely on being joined when we spoke; and we would have our "experiment" to pay attention to even when the formal content of the meeting was dull.

There was a significant increase in the energy in the department as we made the decision to experiment with creating a subgroup system in the all-staff meetings. Department members spoke with enthusiasm about going into these meetings as part of a "team" and reminded each other that "eye contact" was an important part of creating and maintaining functional subgrouping; they made a decision to be conscious of where they sat at the meetings, making sure that they could see each other. One clinician suggested that we name our team "Operation Join," and the name was quickly adopted. Instead of being resigned to the next meeting, we began looking forward to it. Our hypothesis was two-fold: that if we subgrouped we would feel less frustrated or helpless in the meetings; and that we would eventually change the environment of the meetings, and thus have a greater chance of influencing change in the agency.

Launching Operation Join

The next month, we arrived at the all-staff meeting ready to launch Operation Join. Ironically, the CEO had, for the first time, arranged all the chairs in the room in rows facing front and he stood at a table and conducted the meeting. This arrangement was a departure from the more haphazard way in which the chairs were usually arranged in the room and his usual method of choosing a chair randomly. His opening statement, that he thought the classroom arrangement might be more productive, was a clue that he, too, may have been less than satisfied with the all-staff meetings. The arrangement of chairs made it difficult to make eye contact, but the JSO staff made several attempts to join and build. In addition, the atmosphere in the meeting was more tense than usual. Towards the end of the meeting the CEO and one of the other Department Directors began to argue with each other, in the form of sarcasm, "yes-butting" and interrupting each other. The meeting ended leaving the majority of the staff feeling ill at ease at having witnessed this exchange. I left thinking that it was unfortunate that such events occurred on Operation Join's first day and hoped that the next month's meeting would offer us a better start.

I was not prepared for the reaction of my staff later that day. All afternoon, clinicians stopped in my office full of energy and excitement over the meeting. Even though our plan for Operation Join did not do what we had hoped in the meeting itself, the JSO staff had entered the meeting with a very different attitude and with a sense of themselves as members of a system they intended to build and, therefore, were no longer in their unconnected person systems. Being a member of a subgroup system—Operation Join—had provided them with a member system perspective and they were able to apply a multi-level perspective to the events they had witnessed: they were no longer taking the discomfort of the meeting "just personally." In their conversations with me that afternoon, various clinicians noted, with excitement, how the physical structure of the room—with the chairs in rows—affected the atmosphere, how most of the communication was top-down and SAVI red light behavior (see chapter 6), and that they had tracked their own restraining forces for speaking up during the meeting with great curiosity.

Over the next few months, Operation Join began to affect the all-staff meetings. In order to avoid the classroom structure of the previous month, one of the JSO staff offered to set up the chairs for the next month's meeting. The staff member placed the chairs at angles so that from any seat, a person could see about 75% of the others in the meeting. Interestingly the support staff that usually set up the room adopted this new structure for future meetings. As a department, we agreed to sit in different sections of the room so that we changed the norm of people from the same department clustering together and increased our ability to make eye contact with each other. As Operation Join established the norms of joining, building, and commending people, including the CEO, on achievements, more members of the all-staff began to speak up and make comments, especially non-controversial comments. After several months, the meetings had become more pleasant and the tone was lighter, with some laughter. Staff members who had never spoken before were speaking up, especially when they had an occasion to compliment another employee for a job well done. As the JSO staff joined and built on lone voices, others began to follow suit, even when the topics were somewhat controversial.

Learnings from Operation Join

Operation Join—or building a functional subgrouping system—not only had an effect on all-staff meetings, it also increased our JSO cohesion and work energy. We began to discuss "Operation Join" in our department meeting. We would review the all-staff meeting from a systems perspective and then relate what we had learned to our clinical work. Although most of the staff had a working knowledge of many systems concepts, they were now having a shared, live, experience. Our review afforded them an opportunity to subgroup around these experiences which deepened their understanding. They "discovered" anew a number of systems-centered concepts: that there was a difference in their experiences in meetings when they were in member role rather than in person systems; that being aware that they may be a voice for the group helped them to keep a systems perspective and not take things just personally; that joining on similarities changes the environment of the meetings; and that particular behaviors and communication patterns can help us to identify a system's phase of development.

One of the more important learnings in those first few months of the Operation Join experiment was the difference it made as the staff members reduced their flight behaviors and became actively engaged in the meeting. As the JSO staff made eye contact and subgrouped, they shifted from feeling helpless to frustrated. They also learned that frustration itself, especially when contained within a subgroup, was far more pleasant and energizing than the alternative of being "zoned out," "numb," and isolated in flight defenses.

As the staff became more curious about the triggers to their frustration, they began to recognize that the difference between their expectations and the reality of the situation was frustrating. They discovered that frustration was a by-product of super-imposing what SCT calls "maps" or cognitive distortions in place of the reality or the "real territory" of the agency. One of these "maps" was the belief that all-staff meetings should not be frustrating. Because the majority of the employees were generally pleasant in social interactions, the staff had been operating from the assumption that it should be easy to make the meetings pleasant. We explored the SCT hypothesis that "who we are at any particular moment has more to do with the system we are in than our own personal characteristics." The staff began to have a first-hand understanding that we are often controlled by the dynamics of a group, an understanding important for them in their work with the families, victims, and the perpetrators of sexual abuse.

Another "map" that the staff became aware of was the thought that the all-staff meetings should be conducted like the JSO department meetings. They were used to JSO meetings with a leader who had a democratic leadership style, believed in functional hierarchy rather than authoritarian hierarchy, and created a norm of functional subgrouping so that the differences became resources for the group rather than triggers to conflict. So of course they found it unpleasant to shift gears into the more constricting atmosphere of a meeting led in an authoritarian style. But as unpleasant as the shift was, the staff began to recognize that being aware of the shift in context—and coming into the reality of the all-staff meeting fully aware of all its frustrations—was better than experiencing the surges of outrage each time something in the all-staff meeting didn't match the ideals that the JSO department was striving for.

Hitting the Turbulence

During its seventh month, Operation Join experienced a significant challenge as the CEO brought in a mixed message, that our financial status was good and simultaneously that things would be tough for a while and require extra work.

This speech was met with several moments of silence, and then members of Operation Join became very active. However, instead of paying attention to the goal of creating an atmosphere conducive to joining, the members reacted to the mixed message. Full of frustration, they tried to decipher the real information behind the ambiguities and contradictions. They started asking the CEO direct, narrow-ended questions about the financial state of the agency and the stability of their jobs. As his answers became increasingly vague, the clinicians "joined" each other by adding more questions. They also started pointing out the contradictions in his statements. They were anxious, angry and frustrated, and although their tone was respectful, they could not contain their impulse to ferret out information.

Alarmed and concerned about the type of behavior that Operation Join had exhibited in the meeting, I spent the next few days, personally reviewing the history of Operation Join and examining whether I had contributed to the staff's publicly taking on the CEO at the all-staff meeting. Had I induced the members of my department to act out my authority issue with the CEO? Had I placed members of my department in jeopardy by encouraging them to participate in Operation Join and behaving outside the norms of the agency? Had I failed to emphasize the real differences between the context of the larger agency and that of the JSO department, so that the clinicians were not fully aware of the possible consequences of behavior beyond the pale of the agency norms and too different to be supported by the agency?

At the next department meeting, I asked the department members if they thought that Operation Join had moved into fight (SCT works with fight as the second phase in system development). At first, the staff adamantly denied any awareness of fight. Finally, one staff member said that she did know she had been very frustrated and was determined to get a clear answer about the agency's status, "no matter what." Gradually, the others became aware of how they had turned frustration and fear into fight energy. One member commented that Operation Join had transformed from "cheerleaders to the offensive line." I was able to join them by recognizing that I, too, had experienced much frustration, aggression, and anxiety. Once we were aware of how the fight was a response to the high levels of frustration we were trying to manage, I was able to normalize their fight behavior—whereas others in the room had gone into the more common flight defense, members of Operation Join, were the ones who were experiencing the frustration. Because we had been subgrouping functionally and supporting each other from going into our previous behaviors of "zoning out" or going "numb" we were much more susceptible to the discomfort of the frustration. From an SCT perspective, this increase in energy—even if it was fight energy—was a driving force for system development. The awareness of frustration in relation to the actual context indicated we were no longer in the flight phase and instead were relating to the reality of the agency. The next challenge, instead of going into fight with the CEO, was to contain the frustration and use the energy to take up our roles in the all-staff meeting.

Using the SCT Framework of Role, Goal, and Context

First, we looked at the larger agency as the context in which we were working. We recognized that the context was work, with real power differentials and the goal of providing good clinical services. We also discussed how the agency existed in the larger context of the mental health field which was now being funded by managed care companies and that services were being reimbursed at a lower rate which weakened the financial health and the stability of the agency. Looked at in the larger context, our role as employees was to provide good clinical services, to meet our utilization rate, and to document our services so that we could continue to pass audits and receive funding. Feeling good about our jobs and liking the agency were irrelevant unless our performance was affected. As we looked at our roles in this context, we became aware that we had data to support our excellence in achieving the clinical and financial goals. However, we were taking our experience in the agency "personally," and were reacting with frustration to many of the forces interfering with our satisfaction of working at the agency. For example, within the context of the larger agency, the norm at meetings was disengagement rather than engagement, a top-down pattern of communication, and vague or contradictory communication patterns that obstructed the transfer of information. Once we became clear about the larger picture of the managed care environment, we were able to "de-personalize" the CEO's reluctance to be explicit about the financial difficulties of the agency. We also became aware that we had a choice of whether or not to take the norms of the larger context entirely personally and that if we did not take them, and the accompanying frustration, just personally, we had an opportunity to resonate not only with the CEO who was in a difficult position, but also with our adolescent clients. As adjudicated sex offenders, they, too, were the recipients of authoritarian communications (from the court, probation officers, case mangers) and were both the recipients and the initiators of obscure communication patterns.

Next, we looked at the goals of the all-staff meeting, and identified both the implicit and explicit goals of these meetings. (SCT discriminates between the explicit goals which are those that are overtly stated and the implicit goals which can be inferred from behavior.) Although the stated, explicit goal was to inform the employees of the progress, problems, and news of the agency, the implicit goal was to keep out information that would raise employees' questions or concerns. The meetings were "as if," with the CEO and CFO "disappearing" behind redundant, ambiguous, or contradictory statements that obscured information. The staff, who were physically there, would also "disappear" by zoning out. As a department, we looked at how the mutual "disappearance" contributed to the homeostasis of the agency, by protecting the staff from problems and preventing engagement with, or solution to, the difficulties that the agency was facing. We then looked at the goals of Operation Join and explored if we were also working towards implicit goals that were negatively affecting the achievement of our explicit goal of creating a supportive subgroup in the agency to contain the frustrations. As we explored our experiences in Operation Join, we realized that despite our intent to form a supportive subsystem, we were also acting out our authority issues with the CEO by "showing" him how to run a meeting and by using our system to support each other in confronting him at the meetings. Whereas our intent had been to create a friendlier, more open environment, we had inadvertently started using our "muscle" in reaction to what we had interpreted as the "muscle" or power that the CEO and CFO were flexing by being evasive or contradictory. To our chagrin, we were, indeed, part of the system! From that discovery, we were able to recognize how we were re-enacting the overt compliance/covert defiance pattern that our adolescent clients often displayed in groups.

We then looked at our own roles in the agency and questioned whether the role of employee, clinician, and member of Operation Join were congruent or contradictory roles. As we explored this question, we became aware of how our "maps" or "should's" were restraining forces to making these roles congruent. Although we had previously differentiated our "maps" of the all-staff meetings from the department meetings, we had not been successful enough in differentiating our clinical roles from our employee roles—*we were still clinging to our clinical roles in the non-clinical context of the all-staff meeting* in that we were being critical that the all-staff meetings were not similar to the systems that we had created in our clinically focused department meetings and with our clients. And although we had created Operation Join to manage the frustration of the all-staff meetings, we were not fully in the context of those meeting as we still had "one foot" in our clinical roles. As we explored our roles in Operation Join, we became aware that we had been using "Join" as an implicit message to others to "Join us in our behavior" rather than "Let us fully join the actual system of these meetings." We explored the implications of not fully joining the larger system and discovered that, by keeping ourselves removed, we were *adding to rather than defusing* the defensive atmosphere. Despite our joining behavior, we could not be fully supportive of a system that we had only partly joined.

Next, we took a look at the restraining forces against fully taking up our employee roles. What we discovered was that, while committed to our clinical roles, we were not fully committed to this agency. We had ignored our dissatisfactions by identifying ourselves solely as clinicians in the JSO department and avoided relating as agency employees. We began to gain an awareness of the difference between being a clinician and an employee. We also gained an awareness of a choice—*who* we are as clinicians is different from *where* we choose to practice as clinicians. As the clinicians became aware of their freedom to decide whether this was the agency in which they wanted to work, they felt less helpless. They wanted to see if they could both maneuver themselves within the agency to get what they wanted and influence the system to be more supportive of their work

Once it was explicit that the context of the all-staff meeting was generally defensive, that its implicit goal was to keep much important information out of the meeting, and that we were not yet fully in our employee roles, our pathway became clear. Instead of trying to change the system—or any one person in the system—it was our job to acknowledge that we *were* part of the system and to fully take up our roles in that system. Our job now was to create a supportive environment—*which included supporting and subgrouping functionally with the CEO*—instead of focusing on and targeting the agency's defenses.

Through Operation Join, we had taken the first step in supporting each other to become fully present at the meetings. We had also been successful in creating a pleasant, lively atmosphere during those meetings when there was little or no conflict. Our next step was to take our roles as employees, to contain our frustration when conflict did arise, and to modify our reactions to the frustration. Instead of expecting the realities of the agency to change, our job was to change the ways we managed our reactions to these realities and keep finding ways to influence the agency as an employee. And, in our employee roles, each person's job was also to collect data about whether or not the agency was functioning well enough to support each individual employee in his or her clinical role.

Taking the Next Steps

During the next few months, Operation Join took on a different tone. Members explicitly supported the CEO at meetings—often a member sat next to the CEO—members consciously used "I" statements instead of questions, and, using eye contact, helped each other to contain impulses and slow down the pace of the meeting so that they were able to respond by joining rather than reacting too quickly with discharges. Outside of the meetings, the JSO staff became more proactive in addressing problems with employee benefits and with agency procedures that interfered with their ability to function as clinicians. When met with frustration, they reminded each other that *frustration is information* about the level of functioning of the agency and that such information was what they needed in order to make decisions about continuing to work at this agency. In the meantime, rumors of financial disaster were becoming more frequent in the agency, but there were, as yet, no facts available to support or refute those rumors.

Eventually, we did discover that the rumors about our shaky finances were true and that the agency was being acquired by a larger organization. For the acquisition to take place, however, the agency needed to trim its budget, and management positions, including mine, were eliminated. Although the department members were shocked, angry and upset, I believe the work we had done with Operation Join had prepared them to deal with my departure. For ten months, the JSO staff had practiced opening themselves to their responses without taking them "just personally" and had developed an ability to think in a multi-systems way.

At a final department meeting, the staff explored their sense of "betrayal" of me if they continued to work at the agency. Again, we focused on role and context, and they recognized that "betrayal" was in what SCT calls "person system" and that in their clinical role, the top priority was the clinical work, despite their personal feelings or dissatisfaction in their employee role. The real betrayal would be to let their personal feelings interfere with the clinical work. As a group, we also explored the way that we had created a functional, supportive system in the department and how the staff could continue to build these systems with each other and with their clients—they were no longer dependent on the external structure of the department; they had internalized the basics of a systems-centered relationship and could replicate it with their clients. Finally, we looked at how Operation Join could function independent of a particular department, and that they had created a system among themselves that was not dependent on me as the director. Their excitement built as they explored ways that they could take Operation Join into their new situation and use this functional subgrouping system to support themselves and the new director as the new team was forming. One of the staff told me at the end of the day that she had dreaded our last department meeting, expecting it to be a "cry fest" but instead came away full of hope.

Conclusion

One year after leaving the agency, I am still in touch with a number of the staff who worked in my department. Several have made well-considered decisions to leave, and others report that Operation Join has been very helpful in helping them to separate their role of employee from their role as clinician. Members of Operation Join continue to support and contain each other and to remind each other that the goal of being at the agency is to work with the clients. They have become pro-active, setting up a peer supervision group when dissatisfied with the quality of supervision provided by the agency. They also report that they continue to practice Operation Join in all-staff meetings and have added new members to the team. By helping more people to see the reality of the agency, Operation Join has grounded them in the here and now of the full context of the agency and has provided them with a supportive subsystem to contain the frustrations of that context.

We started Operation Join with the goal of changing our work environment; in the process, we changed ourselves. We discovered that it is not important that the "location" be perfect or even desirable; what is important is that we become firmly located in the reality of any workplace so that we can accurately assess these realities and their effect on our clinical work. In many ways, the conditions in this agency have continued to worsen, but the staff who have chosen to stay have made a clear choice to do so. They are no longer in dependent, helpless, complaining roles. They are managing the tough realities of their current context with the goal of finding pathways to reach their full potential, just as they are supporting their clients to do the same.

5

Opening up the Circle: Next Steps in Group Work for Clinical Pastoral Educators

Joan Hemenway, D. Min., Yale University

Clinical pastoral education (CPE) is an educational methodology that combines knowledge of psychology (who we are) with knowledge of theology (what we believe) with process education (how we learn) in order to prepare seminarians, clergy and qualified lay people to provide effective interfaith spiritual care amidst the religious and social complexities of the modern world. Similar to other professional practicum, CPE is offered in a variety of institutional settings—medical centers, nursing homes, prisons, rehabilitative facilities, hospices, counseling centers and local faith communities. Clinical pastoral education programs are supervised by educators (CPE supervisors) who are ordained clergy or ecclesiastically endorsed chaplains trained in psychology, educational theory, and group dynamics.[1]

The CPE educational methodology is based on an action-reflection-action model of learning (Hall, 1992). It includes weekly teaching seminars with an emphasis on theory combined with student case presentations that emphasize application. A key educational element is the small process group involving anywhere from three to eight participants. This group experience, usually quite intense and memorable, is a required element of every accredited clinical pastoral

---

1. CPE Supervisors are certified, and training centers accredited, by the Association for Clinical Pastoral Education, 1549 Clairmont Rd., Decatur, GA 30033 (www.acpe.edu). There are 392 training centers and 685 certified supervisors in the United States (ACPE annual report 2003). There are a number of training centers and supervisors in foreign countries as well.

education program. By seeking to harness the full potential of the small process group experience, students are better prepared not only to engage in significant human relationships but also to understand organizational and systems dynamics in an increasingly complex world.

Hypothesis and Six Examples

It is the hypothesis of this article that the theory and methods of the systems-centered (SCT) group work pioneered by Yvonne Agazarian can make a substantial contribution to CPE group process work. Though this application is still in its infancy, there is evidence of growing interest among CPE supervisors.[2] Not only can SCT enhance our educational efforts, it can also further the implementation of values that the Association for Clinical Pastoral Education considers fundamental to its educational mission.

This article focuses on six specific questions regarding CPE process group work—questions that have been a longstanding focus for conversation among CPE supervisors. The article will demonstrate how SCT group theory and methods can shift the concerns that have elicited these questions from being sources of confusion and misunderstanding to being opportunities for new learning and satisfaction for both CPE students and supervisors.

1) What is the purpose of the small process group in CPE? This question has persisted among both CPE students and CPE supervisors over the years evoking a broad range of responses. It is "an opportunity to develop interpersonal relationship skills," "a context in which to share personal information and feelings," "a place to create an emotionally supportive community and review our pastoral work," "an opportunity to learn about group dynamics and group leadership," and "a context in which to deal with family dynamics and authority issues." No matter what the answer to this question is, or whether the group is highly structured or totally unstructured, a point usually occurs in about the third week of a training unit when an uncomfortably long silence descends on the group with all eyes on the floor. Eventually the most anxious (and courageous) member says (with a short intake of breath and a look of fleeting concern edged with annoyance) "I don't know why we're here."

---

2. At the present time there are approximately 12 CPE Supervisors who have had direct contact with SCT training events. An introductory workshop on SCT subgrouping was presented at the 2003 ACPE Annual Conference. Yvonne Agazarian ran an all-day workshop at the 2004 ACPE National Conference.

One supervisory response to this situation is to refer to the student handbook (every program has one) where there is usually a brief, generic and not very helpful description of this element of the educational program and its purpose. One student reading this description out loud to the group (and the supervisor—perhaps—responding to questions) may or may not move things forward at this juncture. Another supervisory response is to repeat, perhaps more slowly, whatever words of wisdom were initially outlined back at the start of the program about the purpose of process group work in CPE: "We're here to share personally, relate interpersonally, and learn about group dynamics" or some similar version. A third response is to ignore the question and instead comment on the here-and-now dynamics: "I'm wondering how group members are feeling about the long silence in group today?"

There is continued discussion in CPE about how to deal with the inevitable increase of anxiety and resistance in the group. In general, a CPE supervisor working out of the psychoanalytic model/Tavistock tradition (less apparent structure and more confrontive) will make group-oriented interpretations that focus on the group dynamic and not on individuals in the group: "The group in its silence is acting out its anger towards the consultant and has appointed one person to be its messenger (delivered by the supervisor with an unreadable facial expression and their eyes looking at no one in particular)." At the other end of the spectrum, a CPE supervisor working within the humanistic psychology model/T-group tradition (more obviously structured and supportive) will demonstrate relationally available behavior by responding from the perspective of someone inside the group: "I was feeling more anxious as the silence deepened; it would probably be helpful if we each could share how we are feeling (the supervisor looking hopefully around the group at each person)." No matter which supervisory approach is taken, or all the variations in between, students basically experience group work in CPE as "group therapy"—a designation that has prompted considerable dialogue among CPE supervisors through the years (Hemenway, 1996).

SCT has at least two specific contributions to make to this conversation. First, SCT's emphasis on role, goal and context immediately clarifies that CPE is first and foremost a professional education program intended to prepare qualified lay people, seminarians and clergy to deal with the intricacies and intensity of interfaith pastoral work. Though the group educational element may have some therapeutic and personal benefit to participants (that is, it may result in some degree of emotional and behavioral change), the context is educational, the role of the student is to be a member of the group, the role of the supervisor is to be a facilitator of the group, and the purpose of the group's work is to encourage participation in, and reflective observation on, the group experience. Thus, from the SCT perspective, a response to the student's query "I don't know why we're here" might be: "Would you like to explore what you think the goal of the group is and see who can join you?"[3]

Secondly, SCT has built on Kurt Lewin's concept of the group as a "laboratory for learning," an idea familiar to most CPE supervisors. In this theoretical framework, the work of the facilitator is to encourage students to participate in the group (SCT calls it "staying curious on the edge of the unknown") as well as observe and reflect on their participation (SCT: turn on your "inner researcher").[4] Contrary to the early years when CPE supervisors tended to keep the group purpose as mysterious and vague as possible, increasingly it is recognized that students need to learn about group dynamics in order to participate knowledgeably and productively in the group process. SCT emphasizes that setting up specific structures including consistent meeting room, chair arrangement, and clear time boundaries is of the utmost importance. Finally, it is important to note the way a foundational or beginning SCT group starts (with ten minutes of teaching) and ends (with ten minutes of surprises, learnings, satisfactions, dissatisfactions and discoveries).[5] In addition, the initial "distraction exercise" serves as an important means of moving from the person role to the member role.[6] All of the above suggestions are ways "the lab" is provided with sufficient air, light and equipment to assure a comfortable and trustworthy space for the work of learning (and changing) to begin.

2) Is there an alternative to getting stuck in the "hot seat" dynamic? This is an all too familiar pattern in CPE groups where the specific troubles or personal needs or learning problems of one student become the focus for the group. In the early days of process group work, putting pressure on one person (repetitively if necessary) was acceptable and expected in CPE. The rationale for this "hot seat" approach became a cliché: "A group can only go as fast as its slowest member." Though there is growing awareness in recent years of the dangers of this dynamic within groups (creating an identified patient or scapegoat), it continues to be all-too-easy trap to fall into. Though CPE supervisors do offer many instances of

---

3. See question 2 on subgrouping.
4. The use in SCT of colloquial (rather than pathological or psychologically technical) language makes SCT both accessible and user-friendly.
5. Some programs add "applications to pastoral work" here as well.
6. See question 4 for the development of this distinction.

important role modeling in terms of interpersonal relating when dealing with a "problem student" or a "student problem" in the group, it is also a temptation to be drawn into experiencing the pleasure of simply demonstrating one's supervisory skills in front of the group. In addition, students are inevitably drawn towards their desire "to be helpful and comforting," a desire already deeply internalized among those who aspire to the pastoral role.[7]

SCT has made a major contribution in solving this problem through functional subgrouping.[8] By training group members to say "Anyone else?" after each person has made a contribution, and by expecting group members to respond and build on what has been shared, the focus on one person can be alleviated. This is particularly important in the early stages of the life of the group when CPE students may be unsure of the purpose of the group and feel increasingly ambivalent or suspicious about the whole enterprise. The second step to increase the effectiveness of subgrouping is to teach the Push, Wave, Row Exercise (Agazarian, 1997, pp.54-59). This will help CPE students understand the difference between keeping distance and really engaging on a feeling level (rowing).[9] The following example from students working in a hospice illustrates these points:

---

7. See question 3 on clergy role locks.
8. CPE has also placed much value on the development of interpersonal relations among the students, including the ability to give helpful feedback about both personal and professional functioning. The SCT subgrouping approach, though building close emotional connection between people in the here-and-now, does not explicitly focus on communicating specific interpersonal feedback about one's participation in the group; nor does it allow much room for direct negotiation of difficulties in a specific relationship early in a group's development. Rather SCT sees the work of feedback as more relevant in the intimacy phase of group development and after the interpersonal role locks have been weakened so that feedback is not used for ammunition (as it would be in the authority phase) or comes from the perceptions of the role locks. The opportunity to express satisfactions, disappointments and so on at the end of each group session often contains this material for the group until the group is developed enough to work with the interpersonal role tensions. Another helpful SCT tool (adopted from Lewin) is the Force Field Analysis. Here specific data (verbal and non-verbal interventions, tone of voice, metaphors, suggestions, etc) are elicited from group members about which forces were helpful to the group process (driving) and which held it back (restraining). This is sometimes a very effective way to debrief from a particularly intense session and will offer clues into the dynamics of important personal and interpersonal behaviors and relationships.

Student A: I am so upset about Mrs. S. dying. She was such a beautiful person. I couldn't even talk with the family afterwards. I just had to leave the floor (crying). I really need help with this. I know I have a problem...(nods of agreement all around the group)
Student B: When did this happen? [a question is a push]
Student A: Earlier this afternoon (more tears).
Student C: You couldn't even take care of the family? [another push]
Student B: It's probably because the patient reminded you of your mother. [speculative analysis is a push]
Student A: Hmmmm (looking at the floor and disengaging)
Student D: (concerned) I had a similar experience last year in my parish [this effort to identify from past experience is a wave from the shore]
CPE supervisor: There is a lot of focus on questions to A or opinions about A, yet the job here is to join A. Has anyone else had a favorite patient die during this time and could you share your feelings and make eye contact with Student A?
Student E: (after some silence) Well...I remember Mr. B. He was such a faithful man. When he died I just couldn't believe it. I went up to the floor and his bed was empty (looking at Student A). Then I felt an emptiness clear down to the soles of my feet. And a dark sadness sort of took me over... [sharing a here-and-now experience and the feelings attached to it is getting in the boat and rowing with the person]
Student A: Sadness, yes. And I also felt helpless and my arms felt limp [continues to row identifying both emotional and physical feelings]
CPE supervisor (prompting by looking toward Student A): Anyone else?
Student A: Oh yeah, anyone else?

SCT makes an important distinction between functional and stereotype subgroups. Based on a dominant/subordinate dynamic, a stereotype subgroup enforces social stability by rejecting, and even persecuting differences, with some people "in" and others "out." It is this phenomenon that has earned subgrouping a justifiably negative reputation in the group dynamics field. It occurs when two or three of the same people begin to eat together or meet regularly outside of group time, closing off the possibility of changing membership; or members within a group band together on a stereotype similarity like age or sex. A functional subgroup, always working in the context of the group session itself, is constantly integrating differences (taking in new members or new ideas), discovering similarities, and creating greater complexity in their relating in order for the

---

9. A helpful supplement to this learning is the SAVI communication grid in its delineation of red, yellow and green light communication patterns (Simon & Agazarian, 1967; described in Agazarian & Gantt, 2000, pp. 47-69).

group-as-a-whole to survive, develop and transform (Agazarian, 1997). Functional subgrouping also needs to be distinguished from pairing (in which no differences come in) or role locks. Role locks (often unconscious) happen when two people are caught in a repetitive pattern of behavior (often unconscious) and repeat a significant relationship from the past. In one CPE group, a female student and a male student had both gone through recent divorces. Unfortunately they each reminded the other of their former spouses. As a result, they kept the group "entertained" for many weeks during group sessions by constantly nit-picking and criticizing each other whenever the group did not seem to know what else to do.[10] In contrast, functional subgrouping would require anyone feeling the impulse to criticize or nit pick to explore the impulse together in the same subgroup in order that the information contained in the impulse could be integrated into the group-as-a-whole. In this example, both students, and likely others, would end up exploring in the same subgroup together.

3) Do we always have to be nice? The pastoral or religious role carries the burden of a vast array of introjections and projections, and the strong tendency on the part of those who carry these to "take things personally." SCT sees the issue of personalizing as a significant human challenge and an important one for groups to work with. For the CPE student, it is usually introjected parts of significant relationships (including with a personal or impersonal Higher Power) that have most influenced the desire to enter a profession focused on providing spiritual guidance to others. CPE training involves helping students become aware of the kind of introjected material that is shaping both their internal motivation for ministry as well as their external style of doing ministry. Integration of the professional demands *of the role* with personal congruency and satisfaction *in the role* is a crucial step in the educational process.[11]

Of course those in a pastoral role also continually receive whatever projections people in a particular context may decide to express, either indirectly or directly. It is a common experience for a new chaplain intern to approach a nursing station and suddenly all the staff milling around behind the desk stop talking. Several weeks later, after the chaplain has gotten to know the staff, someone may give voice to the feelings behind the (now former) silence: "Okay everybody, let's hold up on the dirty jokes because the chaplain is here!" An important part of CPE

---

10. In Wilfred Bion's terminology, this was a Basic Assumption Pairing Group.
11. SCT would call this "the person-as-a-whole system that contains all the role subsystems, including the centered system which is where the heart is!" (Agazarian, 2003, p.2).

training focuses on helping the student accept and work with such projective material aimed at religious authority in ways that will both contain the feelings generated in the relationships and may eventually lead to exploration of the underlying assumptions.

Work in the small process group includes developing the students awareness of this introjective and projective process within themselves and others. Actively checking out fantasies about peers (which often appear in the form of what SCT calls "mind reads") as well as fantasies about one's self (termed "negative predictions" in SCT), and taking these back[12] in order to establish greater relational reality is particularly important learning. Further, competitive behavior in the group, rather than finger pointing at individuals, can generate strong feelings which, when explored in functional subgroups, releases new energy. In these ways individuals are encouraged to join others in exploring the full potential of their emotional life. This includes accepting the "not-so-nice" parts of themselves along with "the nice" and thus becoming more real.

One group struggled with their negative feelings about another student who was consistently late for group sessions. In this example Student A is twenty minutes late. She enters the room hurriedly, sits down, and addresses the group.

> Student A: (hangs her head and addresses the group): I'm really sorry that I'm late. My floor is really busy and that same nurse wanted to talk to me. I just couldn't say no…(voice trails off as her role lock takes over)
> Student B: (face flushed, right hand in a fist, leaning forward): I was really concerned. I care a lot about you and was worried something was wrong to make you late…again.
> Student C (to Student B): You look angry [mind read]. Are you? [checks it out]
> Student B: No, I just care about her.
> Student C: Well, I'm angry. My body feels tense. I might get into trouble for saying this [negative prediction], but I feel like I could just explode.
> Student D: (leg is tapping the floor) I'm with you. I feel very frustrated. This will probably keep happening at the beginning of every group session [negative prediction].
> Student B: I guess I am a little angry, now that you mention it.
> Student E: I don't think it's right to get angry. If we can't be understanding and patient with each other, how can we be real ministers out there?
> Student A: (to student D) I agree with you. As a chaplain intern I want to always be responsive to people's requests and love them no matter what.

---

12. "Eating and digesting" one's projections (when one is ready) is fundamentally "nutritional" and often brings new energy (Hemenway, 1997, Ch.7).

> CPE supervisor: Today we have a "Make Love" subgroup and a "Make War" subgroup (to Student F who tends to stay on the sidelines): Which subgroup do you want to join?

The next steps in this work would involve the supervisor helping each subgroup continue to reality test their negative predictions and their mind reads as well as explore the array of deeper feelings around expressing or inhibiting their feelings of frustration. This work would lead to a beginning realization of the extent to which the students have introjected their own and others' expectations about how they are to feel and act in the pastoral role.

Recent theoretical work in SCT has distinguished between stereotype roles (a role we are locked into from the past or socially determined roles in the present) and functional roles that are more appropriate to the immediate context and expressive of the spontaneous self (Agazarian & Gantt, 2004). Stereotype roles are the result of adaptation to frustration experienced in previous early attachment relationships and in important growing up experiences. Such compromised roles allowed us to stay in relationship despite experiencing the distress of misattunement. SCT is particularly helpful in highlighting the split-second induction of a role lock through noticing even the smallest of physical changes: head bend slightly to one side, one finger tapping, feet shifting on the floor, eyes averted, face drained of color, slumping position, and so on. Such physical changes are often habitual and thus emblematic of an old role. For CPE students it can be freeing to discover that the professional role of pastoral care giver is not limited to, or even bound by, the stereotype roles learned long ago. Being sensitive to those times when the clergy role has actually inducted a patient or parishioner into a stereotype role can also be extremely useful when this can be named and worked through in order to create a more real pastoral relationship.

4) Is there life beyond personal story telling? One of the most highly valued aspects of CPE supervision is learning about each student's personal history and faith journey. Initial material required for application to a program includes a lengthy autobiographical essay. The personal interview prior to acceptance into a CPE program often focuses on examining more thoroughly the texture of a student's relationship to parents, siblings, and influential teachers and spiritual mentors. During the training itself, dynamics with patients are often highlighted in verbatim sessions as being part of the "parallel process" reflected within the student's personal story. For example, a male student whose mother recently died may be overly attentive to the son of a female dying patient, spending extra time without realizing the degree of identification active in his pastoral work until this is pointed out.

In terms of the actual verbal sharing of personal story, the CPE process group often provides the main stage. CPE supervisors working out of the humanistic psychology tradition often begin the first session by telling their own story and thereby modeling "how to do it" for the students. Some programs then devote the next few sessions to each student telling his/her "lebenslauf".[13] Students who have already had therapy bring hard-won insights about family dynamics, often sharing personal problems. Others, more hesitant, struggle with exactly how to deal with this initial up-close-and-personal expectation in CPE. As this process unfolds, the group atmosphere usually appears to become increasingly intimate, cohesive and "covenanted" (bound) together.[14] Unfortunately, when personal story time is concluded, the group is still confronted with trying to figure out its purpose.

The systems-centered approach uses neither the content of each individual's story, nor his/her professional niche, as the main identifier for the person's presence in the group. Taking up one's role as a group member depends less on personal autobiography and more on being able to respond emotionally to whatever the phase of development of the group and whatever material the subgroup is exploring in the here-and-now. Moving out of the person system into the member system in order to "do the work" of the group-as-a-whole marks a critically important shift within one's self and in relationship to the other group members.[15] The crucial first step is training students to become aware of the fork in the road between explaining and exploring (Agazarian 2001, pp.122-123). In summary, the systems-centered approach to process group work requires new learning (knowledge of systems and how they work), leadership (someone who has been trained in SCT group methods), and discipline (the ability to stay curious and "live at the edge of the unknown").

---

13. "Guidelines for Lebenslauf" (compiled by Dr. Glenn Asquith of Moravian Seminary, Bethlehem, PA) used by some CPE supervisors indicates nine areas of exploration including meaning of your birth, early injunctions, major losses and disappointments, major successes and achievement, religious history. The objective is to "discern new meanings of these stories and allow others to relate us with more depth and understanding."
14. More will be said about phases of group development in section 5.
15. For a helpful description with diagrams of this shift see Agazarian and Gantt (2000), pp.90-96.

A middle-aged woman, eldest of two girls, had grown up with a mother who suffered frequent bouts of depression resulting in periodic hospitalizations. As a result, this woman found herself as a teenager caring for her father and younger sister in both practical and emotional ways. Having learned a clear and much-needed role in her family of origin, she was strongly drawn towards the caring and helpful aspects of ordained ministry. However, underneath her responsible and proud self-image was identification with her mother that included deeply held fears of becoming emotionally ill herself.

When this woman first joined an SCT training group, she tended to be inducted into a stereotype role lock whenever any member of the training group became emotionally upset. She would immediately reach out to calm and reassure. Her work in the SCT group was to let go of this immediate emotional response and, instead, access other parts of her feeling life and join the ongoing work of one of the subgroups. Her success at doing this was not only satisfying and emotionally expanding, but also led to the realization that her mother, though ill at times, was in fact a very accomplished professional person. This data from her past significantly eased her fears about her own present and future mental health.

The exciting aspect of SCT for CPE supervisors and students is that this approach quickly frees people from the constructions and constrictions that they have created for themselves through the life-long formulation of their personal story with its stereotype roles. By staying in the emotional reality of the present moment, rather than going to formulations about past hurts and disappointments or future hopes and fears (forms of irreality that SCT calls "explanations"), group members begin to get to know themselves *and* each other in more satisfying, and often unexpected, ways. By no longer taking things "just personally," individual group members begin to see how they are part of the group-as-a-whole and the larger living human system that is striving to survive, develop and transform itself on many levels. For some CPE students, this may initially be a loss, denying them some of their personal satisfactions for entering ministry in the first place; for others this may be a relief that actually frees them to commit more deeply to a pastoral vocation.

5) Does the authority issue ever go away? The brief answer to this question is No! Agazarian writes: "[The authority issue] is as old as the human race and it fuels revolutions and wars. It never sleeps; a leviathan, it stirs restlessly in the depth of human experience and is easily aroused" (Agazarian 1997, p.241). Whether, and exactly how, to deal with the leviathan is one of the biggest challenges for CPE supervisors when leading process groups. In general, this issue seems to be more accessible for those working in the psychoanalytic tradition than it is for those working in the humanistic psychology tradition. And while students are strongly encouraged to exercise pastoral authority in their ministry with patients and in their relationships with other professional staff, they are often given mixed messages in the group—both about initiating confrontation among themselves and about questioning the authority and competence of the supervisor.

Occasionally the process group work in CPE will be videotaped for supervisory peer review, supervisory training, or student learning. The presence of the camera provides an excellent opportunity to surface the authority issue, an opportunity some students assiduously avoid while others take it up with alacrity:

> Student A: I don't like having the camera here. It makes me nervous.
> Student B: I agree. I don't see why it's necessary. Did we do something wrong?
> Student C: It doesn't affect me.
> Student D (glancing anxiously around): Me neither. What shall we talk about?
> Student E: I just had a wonderful visit with one of my patients.
> CPE Supervisor: We have two subgroups, one that is "Camera Ready" and one that is "Camera Shy."
> Student B: Well, I don't feel particularly "ready" but I do feel angry.
> Student A: Me too. It's like someone with a big eye watching us all of a sudden.
> Student B: Spying on us...maybe getting ready to hurt us.
> Student A: I'd like to hurt it, just kick it and knock it down.
> Student C: I don't know why you're making such a big deal of the camera.
> CPE Supervisor (to Student C): You are probably in the "Camera Shy" subgroup. For the moment let's allow the "Camera Ready" group to do some work together before you come in.
> Student D: I don't know which group I'm in.

It is comforting to learn about the seriousness with which SCT takes the authority issue and understands exploration of this issue as key to being able to integrate one's authority into one's self and into one's work role. This is also a central aspect of the learning task and ministry experience in clinical pastoral education.

In SCT the authority issue is carefully enumerated in the many subphases of group development within the Authority phase.[16] It is only by working through the defenses in the authority phase that a group is then ready to move to the defenses of the intimacy phase. Still later comes the emergence of an interdependent work group that has flexibility to explore more deeply aspects within any of the three phases. Thus, defenses are actually restraining forces specific to each phase of group development. They mark the many ways people learn to cope (that is, maintain attachment) despite the inevitable misattunements experienced initially in relationship to primary caregivers and later in relationships with significant others (McCluskey, 2002b). Though the term "defenses" may sound too psychological or therapeutic for many CPE supervisors, the way SCT works with defenses (that is, everyday coping mechanisms) provides an extremely useful framework through which to understand the parallel process between human emotional development and the phases of group development.

It is very easy for CPE process groups, with the help of the supervisor, to create an initial milieu of interpersonal closeness. From an SCT perspective, by doing this, the process group avoids dealing with social defenses, ignores potential conflict, and creates a pseudo-community to shelter themselves in what they fear might be a stressful training situation. In contrast, CPE supervisors who in the initial interview have explored what SCT calls the social defenses against communication or a cognitive defense against anxiety exhibited by the interviewee, will have begun the process of preparing their students for a different kind of work in CPE and in the process group. Examples of the above include such interventions as: "Do you realize you are smiling as you are talking about the death of your brother?" or "Is your uncertainty about CPE because you have already made a negative prediction about what it will be like?" or "You are at a fork between explaining your reasons for choosing CPE or exploring what you don't know yet about your choice, which way do you want to go?"

In terms of group work, when the CPE supervisor stays relatively separate from the student group and comments consistently on the here-and-now group dynamics, strong feelings about authority will be elicited. This supervisory stance opens the way for the group to begin to move through social and cognitive defenses towards the more rigidified role locks inherent in compliant/defiant feelings, including sadism and masochism. Underneath this material resides the primal rage at authority. This work can be emotionally draining when engaged directly, though when explored using functional subgrouping, the group containment makes it possible to explore the authority struggles.

One CPE group created nicknames for everyone. A tall attractive Afro-American male was King Tut. An outspoken Episcopal woman was "Miss Piss." A

---

16. "The dynamics of the authority issue are *the fulcrum dynamics of the process of change* (my italics) in all human systems, from simple to complex" (Agazarian, 1997, p.241).

Roman Catholic Sister who was terribly nice and always dressed in a habit was "Snow White." The leader of the group, an Episcopal laywoman, came to be known as "The General." And the CPE supervisor was named "Old Hawkeye." In this particular group, the supervisor sat in a swivel chair that was the best chair in the room. One day the Roman Catholic Sister, at the encouragement of the other students, sat in that chair just before the process group meeting. When the supervisor walked in, Snow White was politely asked to move (which she did). However, the group immediately changed her name to "Sister Act II"!

An approach to CPE group work that consistently and creatively deals with the authority issue requires leadership that is grounded in theory, self-confidence, and curiosity. It also requires ongoing support from colleagues who are engaged in a similar group leadership work. Wilfred Bion left the group dynamics field because he became emotionally worn out with having to sit "behind his face" day after day and contain the projections of his patients (and presumably the staff as well) at the Tavistock Clinic. Experiencing one's own essential loneliness while receiving, but not taking personally, both impassioned idealizations and/or rebellious hatred from group members requires discipline and grit.[17] Being able to return projections (give feedback) in bite-sized digestible pieces that can nourish change and bring new energy within each CPE student requires good timing and accurate attunement. The goal here is to help CPE students give up the defense of externalization (my problems are your fault or my parents' fault or my religious judicatory's fault), so that the path is opened for taking greater responsibility (I can do something to change myself and my behavior) and, therefore, engage more fully in the CPE learning process.

6) How much difference is too much difference? It is currently a high value in the Association for Clinical Pastoral Education to provide training for ministry that is multi-faith and multicultural. This commitment marks a shift from the personal and individualistic approach of former years to a social and contextual frame as the starting point for the pastoral care and clinical pastoral education field in the 21st century: "...spiritual care and the teaching of it should not be viewed as a simple matter of practice by well-intentioned individual practitioners. Rather, it must be seen as a complex cultural practice that has implications for individuals, organizations and society at large" (Lee, 2003, p.5). The seriousness

---

17. Agazarian dedicates her theory book to her brother Jack (1915–1945) "who died for his values, and whose stubborn courage I remember when I am running short of my own" (Agazarian, 1997, frontispiece).

with which this issue is being taken is reflected in the current revising of ACPE standards.[18]

A systems-centered understanding of group dynamics (and indeed of the other educational elements in CPE as well)[19] makes a major contribution in terms of supporting this shift and developing its implications. Systems-centered thinking makes explicit the inter-dependent relationship within the living human system between the group-as-a-whole system, the subgroup system, and the member system. Not only does this approach help students understand their own emotional life more fully (that is, the subsystems within themselves) and contribute to the functional subgrouping work (places where they can be joined by others), but it also helps them "see" the various larger systems (group-as-a-whole, hospital, faith group, local community) in which they seek to do ministry. Further, SCT emphasizes that the work is *always focused* on exploring differences in the apparently similar and the similarities in the apparently different. In this way, groups (systems, organizations, societies) survive, develop and transform themselves.

A CPE group of students had just begun a full-time unit of training. There were two male and two female students from a mainline Protestant seminary, plus a female Jewish rabbi, and a Hispanic Pentecostal man in the group. On the third day of the program, when the group was still in its honeymoon stage, the rabbi turned to the Pentecostal and said: "Do you believe that the only way to God is through Jesus Christ?" Immediately the group went silent. The Pentecostal, ruffled but able to recover, responded: "Do you believe that Jews are the Chosen People?" Both locked eyes while the rest of the group held its breath.

Could the group hold this much difference so early in its life together? Or, would either the rabbi or the Pentecostal (or both, in which case they would form a subgroup) move into a barrier experience of shame and be cut off from his/her spontaneous self and from the group-as-a-whole? Agazarian writes: "System response to the too different is to contain it in a subsystem behind impermeable boundaries which keep it split away from the system-as-a-whole, unless or until the system-as-a-whole develops the capacity to recognize and integrate it" (Agazarian, 2003, p. 4). This is the well-known elephant-in-the-room phenomenon, the secret no one wants to talk about, which can stall all efforts to do the subgrouping work and cause the group to go dead-in-the-water.

---

18. ACPE Draft of 2005 Standards on www.acpe.edu
19. A workshop at the 2004 ACPE National Meeting offered by four CPE supervisors with SCT training focuses on "Designing a Systems-Oriented CPE Curriculum."

The story of the group described here working with their differences actually has a happy, though quite unexpected, resolution. Though they did some good work in the process group as part of the educational program, the real turning point came when they discovered that they could sing in four-part harmony together. Because of obvious religious differences, they initially compromised by singing Broadway songs. However, eventually they developed a repertoire of semi-religious songs in Spanish, Hebrew, and Latin and a few old favorites in English such as "Amazing Grace." Every Friday afternoon the "Singing Chaplains" went to the floors to serenade patients, families and staff with their beautiful music!

Conclusion

These responses to six key questions demonstrate that SCT theory and practice can substantially inform and enrich CPE group process work. One of the most appealing aspects of SCT is its integration of a wide variety of theoretical approaches: general systems theory, communication theory, developmental psychology, cognitive and behavioral psychology as well as the psychoanalytic tradition. This comprehensive approach is consistent for many supervisors in CPE who both appreciate a wide variety of psychological and educational theories and also yearn for ways to bring them all together.

A second appeal of SCT is its emphasis on the integration of the apprehensive (intuitive, emotional) and comprehensive (cognitive) self. Such integration of head and heart lie at the center of clinical pastoral education (Hall, 1992). Increased permeability between these two basic aspects of the human personality results in the ability to mobilize and release one's full resources and energy for ministry. Learning how to fully "use the self" is exciting work! A sign of this achievement is the ability to access one's common sense (an ego free of defenses) in managing day-to-day living as well as major decision-making. As this work takes place in the subgroup and in the group-as-a-whole, the outcome is greater flexibility, creativity and vivacity within the self and in relationships with others.

A third appeal of SCT is its emphasis on empathic attunement as the basis for work in the subgroup. Attunement is defined as "an interpersonal process that takes place between two people based on the communication of verbal and non-verbal signals" (McCluskey, 2002a, p. 2). The importance of eye contact, physical posture, skin tone, facial expression and emotional availability all contribute to effective attunement with another person in an SCT group. This is an experience that potentially heals previous misattunements and the defensive emotional maneuvers that have grown out of these early experiences. From an SCT perspective, this work echoes throughout the living human system that both holds the work and is changed by it as well. Such healing relational work also lies at the very center of pastoral care and clinical pastoral education.

In summary, this chapter discusses how SCT can be useful in strengthening and clarifying the process group component in the CPE educational process. Though the six questions discussed here are central for CPE group work, it is unlikely these questions are unique to CPE alone. In fact, the early interest we have elicited in pioneering SCT in the CPE context suggests that SCT may contribute significantly to any educational process where experiential learning is the primary methodology.

6

Red, Yellow, Green: Modifying Communication Patterns in an Elementary School System

Claudia Byram, Ph.D., Consultant
Edward Marshall, Ph.D., Greene Street Friends School
Anita Simon, Ed.D., SAVI Communications

Realization of educational goals is dependent on the behavior of the people implementing those goals. In this chapter we describe a model for monitoring and modulating verbal communication, an important aspect of implementation behavior. We present action research on introducing the SAVI model (System for Analyzing Verbal Interaction) to the faculty of an elementary school as an aid in responding to discipline issues. SAVI provides teachers with a descriptive picture of their communication interactions with students, and points out alternate communication pathways. Anecdotal data collected from teachers almost two years after the introduction of SAVI is discussed from the perspective of the theory underlying the model.

This chapter spells out an application of Agazarian's systems-centered theory (Agazarian, 1997) in an elementary and middle school whose faculty was interested in developing a deeper understanding of disciplinary situations and more tools to address discipline issues with children. The particular school was Greene Street Friends, a private Quaker school.[1] The particular systems-centered tool that the school imported is SAVI, pronounced "savvy," the System for Analyzing Verbal Interaction. (Simon, 1996b; Simon & Agazarian, 2000). SAVI maps the verbal communication of human systems—how people talk to each other—in a way that permits people to view what they say, and how they say it, descriptively.

---

1. Our thanks go to the participating staff at Greene Street Friends School.

In this chapter we discuss this project, viewing the intervention as a pilot for bringing SAVI—a tool for change—into educational systems.

In 2002, SAVI was introduced to the faculty of Greene Street Friends via a one-day in-service training. The implicit assumption in choosing SAVI was that the way teachers and students talk to each other is a major channel for conflict resolution. Providing teachers with this tool for analyzing how they and students talk to each other in contentious situations would thus be useful in choosing behavior which would help resolve these situations. Looking back nearly two years later, we see that bringing SAVI into the school has had significant effects on the communication behavior of a subset of teachers, specifically on their interaction with children in the classroom and on their approach to discipline. Some teachers also reported that new skills migrated out of the school system and into interactions with family members and social situations. The effects that teachers have reported to us and that we have recorded in this article are relevant to the implementation of larger educational goals and values, and for this reason may be useful to others who are working to put their educational philosophies into practice.

Background of the Project

The faculty at Greene Street Friends School had identified "discipline" as an issue that it wanted to address throughout the school. It had formed a school wide discipline committee charged with looking at resources for helping the faculty as a whole manage discipline issues.

The school head, one of the authors, was familiar with SAVI, and suggested that the discipline committee consider this model as one of the resources available to them. He had found the model useful in his role in handling serious discipline issues, conflicts between teachers and parents and in developing his own communication style.

This discipline committee asked one of the authors to talk with them about SAVI and to discuss what they could expect from a one-day training. They found the idea of SAVI interesting, particularly the author's modeling of SAVI—based strategies. The result of this initial meeting was that the discipline committee decided to offer a one-day in-service SAVI training to the entire faculty.

There is a significant congruence between Friends School culture (Faith and Practice, 1972) and the SAVI approach. First, Friends Schools emphasize individual empowerment, and the SAVI tool can be used by all levels of the system: students, teacher, administration, support staff, parents, etc. Second, Friends Schools focus on the tone of interpersonal communications, and SAVI explicitly observes tone. Third, Friends schools prioritize integrating people into the group, and SAVI operationalizes this idea by describing pathways to reduce conflict and confrontation in passing experiential information from one person or group to another. Fourth, Quaker values emphasize clearness or clarity, and SAVI is explicitly designed to spell out the behaviors which promote clarity in the communications systems as alternatives to those that introduce ambiguity, confrontation or avoidance.

Origins of the SAVI Model

The System for Analyzing Verbal Interaction (SAVI) (Simon & Agazarian, 1967), originated in the 1960's at Temple University. Two graduate students, Yvonne Agazarian and Anita Simon, were investigating the currently available tools and concepts for describing classroom and group behavior (Simon & Boyer, 1971). They were dissatisfied with what they found: they wanted an observation system that would organize the actual behaviors used in the communication process according to criteria based in information theory. The existence of such a tool would allow researchers to study the effects of different kinds of communication behavior on productivity and morale in different settings.

Agazarian had built on Shannon and Weaver's (1964) work which defined noise in the communication system as ambiguity, redundancy and contradiction (Agazarian, 1968; Simon & Agazarian, 1967). Shannon and Weaver formulated an inverse relationship between noise in the communication channel and the probability that the information in the channel will transfer. The result of applying these ideas to verbal communication was SAVI, a system for categorizing any verbal behavior in accordance with 1) its potential for effective transfer of information, and 2) its balance of emotional and topic information (Agazarian, 1968 & 1969).

Figure 1   S A V I ™   G R I D
System for Analyzing Verbal Interaction

	PERSON	FACTUAL	ORIENTING
R E D L I G H T	**1 FIGHT** Attack/Blame 1A Righteous Question 1R Self Defense 1D Complain 1C Sarcasm 1S	**2 DATA-VOID** Mind Reading 2M Negative Prediction 2N Gossip 2G Stories/Joking 2J Thinking Out Loud 2T Ritual 2R	**3 COMPETE** Yes-but 3B Discount 3D Leading Question 3L Oughtitude 3O Interrupt 3I

Y E L L O W L I G H T	**4 SOCIAL SELF**
	
	Personal Info
	   current 4C
	Personal Info
	   past 4P
	Personal
	   Explanation 4E
		5 PUBLIC DATA
		
		Facts and Figures 5F
		General Information 5G
		Narrow Question 5N
		Broad Question 5B
			6 INFLUENCE
			
			Opinion 6O
			Proposal 6P
			Command 6C
			Impersonal
			   Reinforcement 6I

G R E E N L I G H T	**7 EMPATHIZE**
	
	Tells own feelings 7F
	Asks (inner-person)
	   Question 7Q
	Answers (inner-
	   person) Question 7A
	Mirrors Others'
	   Inner experience 7M
	Affectionate Joke 7J
	Self Assertion 7S
		8 DATA PROCESS
		
		Answers Question 8A
		Paraphrase 8P
		Summarize 8S
		Clarifies own Answer 8C
		Corrective feedback 8F
			9 INTEGRATE
			
			Agreement/Positive 9A
			Builds on others
			   Ideas or Experience 9B
			Work Joke 9J

Silence   Laughter   Noise

SAVI ™ is a trademark of Anita Simon & Yvonne Agazarian   © Simon and Agazarian 2002

Red Light behaviors (Figure 1, top row) are noisy behaviors. A conversation using these behaviors, e.g., Attack, Complain, Mind Reading, Leading Questions, will sound like a fight or an argument. From a theoretical perspective we would say that these behaviors contain a high level of ambiguity, contradiction and redundancy. This is what makes it difficult for a listener to get the essence of the speaker's message.

As Agazarian developed systems-centered theory and practice, the SAVI model provided a way of describing communication behaviors and their effect on what gets heard, that is, on how permeable boundaries are to new information.

Although SAVI was developed as a research tool (Browne, 1977; MacKinnon, 1984; Simon & Agazarian, 2000 op. cit.; Sturdevant, 1991; Weir, 1978; Zimmerman, 1970), it has been used most frequently as a practical aid in clinical and organizational work with those for whom verbal communication is an important part of their work and lives (Agazarian, 1972; Simon, 1993; Hughes, 1984; Fellows, 1996; Simon, 1996a).

SAVI: A Brief Description

SAVI is a tool for collecting and analyzing information about what happens when people talk to each other. The communication behaviors which SAVI charts are verbal behaviors such as Commands ("Everyone please take your seat."), Building on Others' Ideas ("I like your idea of inviting the whole faculty and staff to a party. Maybe we could even open it up to spouses and other family members.") Giving Facts ("The printer prints 6 sheets per minute"), Complaints ("There's never any room to park around here!")

SAVI organizes these communication behaviors into patterns that reflect the potential for information transfer, that is, for successfully getting our message across. This collected information can be used to describe a person's, a group's, or a system's current communication patterns. SAVI additionally points to a variety of behaviors which are likely to facilitate better communication.

The framework of SAVI is a 3 x 3 grid, made up of 3 rows and 3 columns, forming 9 squares (See Figure 1 above). Each square contains several categories of similar behaviors. For example, the "Fight" square, Square 1, contains the behaviors of Attack, Blame, Righteous Questions, Self-defense, and Sarcasm.

The horizontal rows of the grid show the information-transfer potential of communication. We use a traffic light metaphor—Red, Yellow and Green behaviors—because just as a red traffic light stops traffic, information stops when it is being carried by Red Light behaviors (Attacks, Mind reads, Yes-buts, Self defense, etc). Similarly, Green Light behavior facilitates the flow of information (Paraphrase, Agreements/positives, Building on others ideas, Sharing own feelings, Summarizing, etc.)

The vertical columns deal with whether the information contained in the communication is primarily about feelings/relationship (Person column) or primarily about topic (Factual and Orienting columns).

Imagine that each time a behavior is used a tally mark is made in the square that contains that category. So if a teacher said "How much is 2 + 2?" The observer would mark a tally in Square 5 (Narrow Question).

Let's see how the coding of behaviors in the grid builds up to give us a pattern of behavior. Take, for example, a teacher wanting to use the discovery method to stimulate her students' higher order thinking. Than imagine a colleague trained in SAVI coding the student and teacher interaction. This is what the coder recorded:

> Teacher: Narrow question (Square 5)
> Student: Answer (Square 8)
> Teacher Narrow question (Square 5)
> Student: Answer (Square 8)
> Teacher: Narrow question (Square 5)
> Student: Answer (Square 8)
> Teacher: Broad question (Square 5)
> Student Answer (Square 8)
> Teacher: Yes but, Discount (Square 3)
> Teacher: Narrow question (Square 5)
> Student: Answer (Square 8)

If the coder made a tally mark in the SAVI grid for each statement, you'd begin to see a build-up in the most-used squares, as in the figure below.

Figure 2

1	2	3 Yes-but / Discount /
4	5 Narrow Q //// Broad Q /	6
7	8 Answer /////	9

We would see a buildup of a pattern in Squares 5 and 8 (specifically Narrow Questions and Answers) that shows at a glance that in this class, the students' memories were being tested with fact or yes/no questions. We also see that when students were asked a Broad Question to expand their thinking, their answer was met with the teacher's discount and his own, dissenting opinion. From this descriptive account, we see that what the teacher was actually doing was quite different from what he intended to do. If in fact he does want to require his students to process higher order cognitive information, he now has a smorgasbord of choices of alternate behaviors to elicit and support his student's efforts. For example, he might choose to support a constructivist or student inquiry mode and ask a Broad Question, followed by Silence until a student responds, Paraphrase the student's answer and then ask another Broad Question to solicit others' comments.

SAVI Alerts

There are certain repeating sequences of communication-disturbing behaviors that are so common that they often do not even draw our attention. SAVI has isolated a number of these, and calls them 'Alerts' because they can alert us to trouble in the communication process itself which, if unchecked, can lead to a decrease in productivity and morale (Simon, 1993 op. cit.; Simon, 1996c). One of the most common Alerts is the "Yes-but, Yes-but" pattern that is familiar to us all. ("Let's move the printer over here." "Yes, but the printer is fragile.") The "Yes-but" pattern is commonplace in the classroom, the playground, staff meetings and workgroups. Most of us by now are so programmed to "Yes-but" behavior that we don't even have to hear what comes next; we "know" that what follows the "but" is going to be a reason not to do what was proposed.

Here are some other common Alerts, with illustrative dialogues:

- *Attack-Attack:*

  "You didn't listen to me," an Attack followed by
  "That's because you gave poor directions to begin with," another Attack.

- *Attack—Self-defense:*

  "We're lost because as usual you didn't listen to me" answered by
  "I was trying to listen to you."

- *Opinion-Opinion—Opinion:*

  "We need the Maslow Curriculum" followed by
  "We can't afford the Maslow Curriculum" followed by
  "We're spending too much money on worksheets" etc.

- *Complaint—Complaint:*

  "They're always complaining about us being late" followed by
  "You'd think they'd do something about this terrible parking problem."

- *Interruption followed by Interruption:*

  (We assume the reader can imagine this!)

When these Alert patterns are replaced by Yellow-Green Light patterns, the emotional climate changes and work energy increases.

Let's look more closely at the "Yes-but, Yes-but" Alert. This is a Red Light pattern that introduces contradiction into the communication: it says "yes" and "no" at the same time without processing either side of the contradiction, the "yes" side or the "but" side. The conversants' resulting attitudes are often what we experience in meetings: "What's the use—this isn't going to go anywhere!" Here is an example:

Paul and Harriet were asked by their principal to pick a site for the next school retreat.

> Paul: Let's have our retreat at a place in the country. I think it would be so good for everybody to have a day away from school, and people wouldn't be being interrupted with day-to-day tasks.
> Harriet: Yes, but that would be so expensive. (Alert—the conversation has moved to Red Light.)
> Paul: Yes, but it might be worth some extra expense if we can come up with some great strategies for solving the problem of…(Alert—the conversation is continuing in Red Light.)

The communication problem here is that it is not yet explicit what part of what Paul said (if any) that Harriet agreed with when she said "yes." We don't even know what part of what he said that she disagreed with when she said "but." And of course, the same thing is true of Paul's response to Harriet. In our experience we have observed an almost universal impulse to "yes-but" something with which we disagree, that is, to offer a token agreement (yes; that's a good idea;

interesting) immediately followed by our disagreement (but), creating a noisy communication!

In the SAVI Grid (see figure 3), their discussion would look like this:

Paul:
    Proposal (P) (let's have...
    Opinion (O) (I think....
Harriet:
    Yes-but (YB) (yes, but expensive...
Paul:
    Yes-but (YB) (yes, but worth it if...

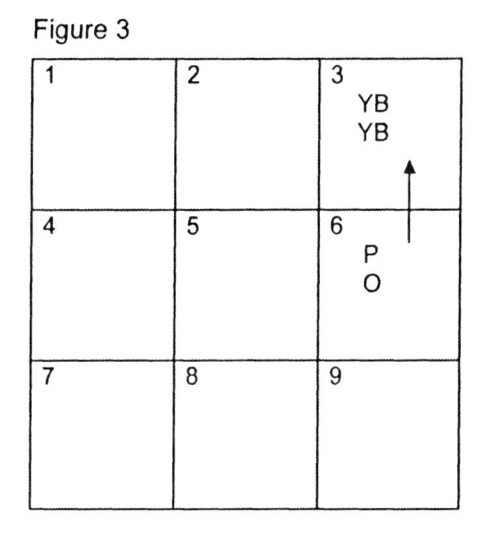

Figure 3

1	2	3 YB YB
4	5	6 P O
7	8	9

We can now use SAVI to create a strategy to improve Paul and Harriet's communication. By strategy we mean a sequence of behaviors selected to meet a communication goal. There are many SAVI strategies for undoing the "Yes-but" impulse in our selves. One that is particularly effective is "Three Builds and a Question": The steps in applying this strategy are:

#1. Catch yourself wanting to "Yes-but" and don't.
#2. Instead, find a Square 9 behavior in yourself—that is, a place where you can honestly "join" with what has just been said. (Agreement or Build), and say that out loud. Repeat the "join" two more times. This is like emotional aerobics—stretching to find the part of yourself that truly is in agreement or has respect for what the other person is saying when a large part of you just wants to disagree.

#3. Ask a real Question (Square 5), not a Leading Question (Square 3), about something you are really curious about that the other person has said.

Here's how this strategy sounded when Harriet thought about trying this 3-step recipe.

> Paul: Let's have our retreat in the country. I think it would be so good for everybody to have a day away from School, and people wouldn't be being interrupted with day-to-day tasks.
> Harriet: That would be really nice. (Agreement #1) The staff did get a lot of work done when we went to a different school to have our retreat last time, because they weren't interrupted. (Build #2) And I agree with you—it would be good for the staff to be away for a day. (Agreement #3) Do you have some ideas about the finances of doing that? (Broad Question)

In the SAVIGrid (see figure 4), this interaction would look like this:

Paul:
    Proposal (P)
    Opinion (O)
Harriet:
    Agreement (A)
    Build (B)
    Agreement (A)
    Broad Question (BQ)

Figure 4

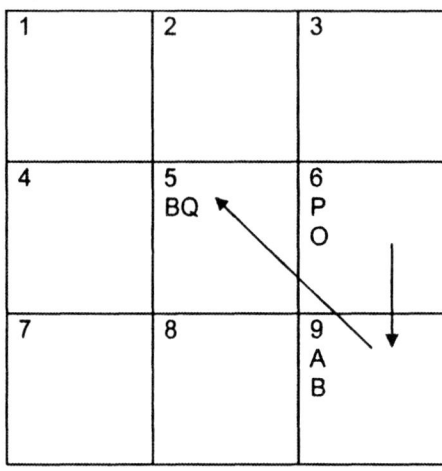

1	2	3
4	5 BQ	6 P O
7	8	9 A B

Harriet used SAVI as a map to guide her in modifying her behavior in the direction of increasing the potential that both her and Paul's messages would get heard. This example of "undoing a Yes-but Alert" illustrates how SAVI functions as a tool to describe communication and as a guide to change it.

Since SAVI is designed to look at the process of communication, that is, the actual verbal behaviors used when anyone is talking to anyone, it can be used to map the current status of information transfer between staff and students, as well as providing a menu of other behaviors to select from to make information transfer more effective. Thus SAVI can be used to both monitor and influence progress toward the major goal of education: learning and growth of students and teachers.

SAVI and the Larger Context of Educational Change

SAVI is a system that describes communication behavior. The actual link between an educational philosophy, policy or curriculum and students is teacher behavior (Flanders & Simon, 1969). Whether one develops and advocates for an educational philosophy (e.g., democracy in the classroom or differentiated instruction) or a school policy (e.g., a discipline policy) or a new curriculum focus (e.g., whole language learning), SAVI points to the communication behaviors that are likely to advance the group in the desired direction, as well as behaviors which create detours and breakdowns.

The SAVI system describes rather than prescribes so that teachers (and students and administrators and support staff and parents if they learn SAVI too) can see if they are doing what they intended to do. It also provides alternatives if the behaviors being used are themselves are blocking movement toward goals.

Data suggest that teachers who were taught a formal system for observing and describing teacher—pupil classroom behavior, modified their own behavior in a positive direction (Amidon & Simon, 1967; Flanders & Simon, 1969; Flanders, 1965). By learning the discriminations needed to use the observation system, teachers had more awareness of their own behavior, and they modified their behavior in the direction of their goals. For example, when teachers learned category systems dealing with higher-order levels of thinking they subsequently used higher levels of questioning behavior and their students used higher levels of cognitive processing (Gallagher, 1966; Rowe, 1986; Redfield & Rousseau, 1981; Taba et al., 1964). In the affective dimension, teachers who studied about behaviors to create a positive classroom climate had students who had greater self esteem, student engagement and increased achievement (Hunt, 1987). Teachers who learned the System of Interaction Analysis (Flanders, 1962) produced more "indirect" teacher classroom behaviors (accepts feeling, encourages, accepts student's ideas and asks questions) and had students with higher achievement (Amidon & Flanders, 1961). The same seems to be true even for teaching mechanical skills (Powell, 1972).

This chapter reports an informal test of the following hypothesis: that the behavioral discriminations that SAVI allowed teachers to make would increase their ability to select behaviors which moved them toward their goals of improved management of 'discipline' situations.

Introducing SAVI to Teachers: An In-service Training

The faculty of Greene Street Friends School attended a one-day SAVI in-service training in the fall of 2002 entitled "Leading with Respect—Answering Disrespect". They were introduced to SAVI through a series of mini-lectures and role-play practices.

As they worked, it became clear that the teachers were using the in-service as an opportunity to talk together about issues they cared very much about, and that the descriptive language of SAVI allowed them to talk effectively about similarities and differences of opinion and experience. They learned about SAVI 'Alerts' (behaviors that can reduce productivity). The staff noted some of the Alerts occurred in faculty meetings (specifically "Yes-but, Yes-but" and "Opinion, Opinion, Opinion") and had a negative effect on the productivity of the meeting. They noted that the communications we "put out" create the public, shared environment. The faculty also used SAVI to process the fact that special teachers (art, music, etc.) had not been included in the planning process for the workshop.

At the end of the day, the group reflected on what they had done. Teachers found using the SAVI grid to be "provocative," "interesting," and "effective." They also noted how much work it takes to communicate effectively and how easy it is to say something that makes communication harder. They were dissatisfied that there was not more time to work on strategies and interactive practice.

Two Years Later

In 2004, 12 of the 20 teachers who attended the SAVI in-service training in 2002were still using it in their thinking about their teaching. Of these 12, three found it a "significant tool" in their work with students and nine reported that SAVI has been "somewhat useful" to them. These results are the product of a very brief training intervention one and one-half years previously, with no formal follow-up training. We were pleased and a little surprised that the small amount of training in SAVI had such durability, and curious about what might result from continued training for interested teachers. Clearly, integrating a system like SAVI into one's teaching repertoire is a process, and one we know little about. In writing this article we were interested in what the teachers who were continuing to use SAVI after a very brief training could tell: what had been useful and what have the rewards been?

In preparing for this article we collected specific anecdotal data about where and how teachers have been using SAVI. We hoped that by looking at the changes teachers made we could assess SAVI's usefulness as a tool to support teachers moving in the direction of their goals. Below are seven teachers' anecdotes about how they have used their SAVI understanding with students. These reports are close paraphrases of what teachers said in interviews with one of the authors. Some details, including names, have been edited to protect confidentiality.

Following each anecdote, we have done a SAVI analysis of the teacher's "crucial behavioral change" that moved the climate from Red/Yellow to Green/Yellow.

Report #1: Teacher of Younger Children

"I asked a student to work on a project, and although he started his work, he did not follow my directions. When I gave him feedback about his project, he was ready to crumple it up and got very frustrated. I restated the directions in a way that was very concrete, and he interrupted, saying, "I already did that." Rather than discounting him, I said, "The directions were [and I repeated the directions]." To my great satisfaction, he stopped arguing, went back, and finished his work. While I did not have the SAVI grid in my mind at the time, I see how he received my most important message, because I did not fight with him, I stuck to the facts, and I kept my tone positive."

SAVI analysis
Teacher (figure 5): Gives Facts (directions)—Square 5

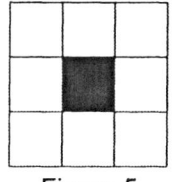

Figure 5

Student (figure 6): Interrupt, Discount ("I already did that")—Square 3

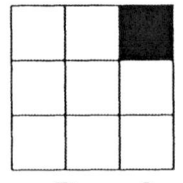

Figure 6

Teacher:
Pre-training (figure 7): Would have joined in Red (Discount—"arguing back")—Square 3

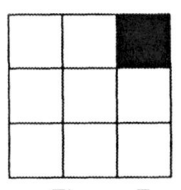

Figure 7

Post-training (figure 8): Gives Facts (repeats directions again, positive voice tone)—Square 5

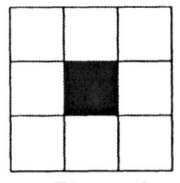

Figure 8

Result: Student went back to work

Report #2: Teacher of Younger Children

"A woman came to our first grade classroom to talk about different ways we handle feelings, encouraging students to talk feelings out, rather than to act them out. She asked students to take turns saying something they liked about themselves, and then to sing a song. Emily was angry, and said she thought the activity

Red, Yellow, Green 113

was "babyish," that the woman didn't understand or know her. Before I had learned about SAVI, I would have tried to cajole Emily (with Oughtitudes, Discounts, and Mind Reads) into changing her attitude about the whole thing 'telling her about her problem' and 'making it better from my point of view.' Instead, after the class I sat down with Emily and asked her to talk about how she felt, given the fact that the woman really didn't know her. Emily stated a number of negative Mind Reads about the woman and began to cry. I suggested that she talk with the woman the next time she came, instead of imagining what the woman was thinking. The woman did come back, and she and Emily calmly talked out Emily's issues."

SAVI analysis.
Student (figure 9): Attack (name calling: "that's babyish!")—Square 1

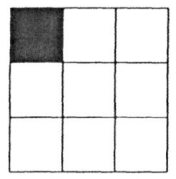

Figure 9

Teacher:
Pre-training (figure 10): Oughtitudes, Discounts, Mind reads—Squares 2 and 3

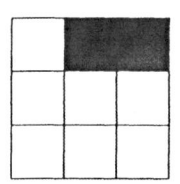

Figure 10

Post-training (figure 11): Asks for feelings, Mirrored Feelings, Proposal—Squares 6 and 7

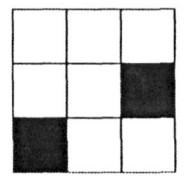

Figure 11

Results: Student accepts teacher's proposal and acts on it.

Report #3: Teacher of Older Children

"Recently, I was teaching a class, and Holly was doodling on her paper. My policy is that doodling is fine if it doesn't physically cover your notes or keep you from taking notes. Holly was doodling on her pants. The next thing I knew, she had drawn with a pen all over her face. At that point, I had a choice. I could get upset and fight with her (I would have used all three squares in the top row of SAVI), or get/give information. When I tried to do this, she challenged me with Red Light expressions, such as "If you hadn't said anything, no one would be looking at me." I said that I wouldn't take the blame and was also careful not to turn the blame back on her. I simply tried to stick to the facts: that the class was distracted, that I wasn't placing blame on her, and that people were turning to look at her, since there was writing on her face. We were able to move past the situation and she did too. Within a minute, we were back to teaching and learning math."

SAVI analysis.
Student: Unacceptable non-verbal behavior.

Teacher:
Pre-training (figure 12): "Would have used all three squares in the top row of SAVI."

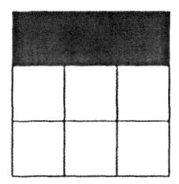

Figure 12

Post-training (figure 13): Gives information—Square 5

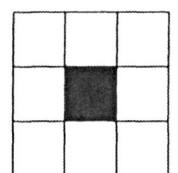

Figure 13

Student (figure 14): Blame ("If you hadn't said anything...")—Square 1

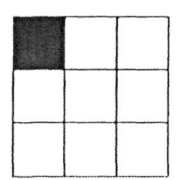

Figure 14

Teacher:
Post-training (figure 15): Gives facts about class process ("You have writing on your face, class is looking at you, class is distracted from its work")—Square 5

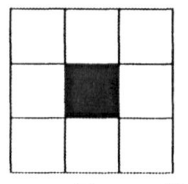

Figure 15

Results: Student and Teacher and Class direct attention back to mathematics.

Report #4: Teacher of Older Children

"Two kids came to me, yelling and screaming at each other. Before learning SAVI, I would have told each of them what they were thinking and asked them to solve their problem. Instead, I set up a scenario, "I notice that there is a conflict. We are going to talk about the conflict. Everyone will get a chance to speak. I want you to use "I" statements. If this were my conflict I would say "I feel attacked when you come up to my face and yell at me." I asked them to not interrupt. At some points I asked clarifying questions. Once they took their turns, I then mirrored back what I heard—restating and summarizing. Then I asked if there were any inaccuracies in the other person's story. They saw that by clarifying a misunderstanding, no one was at fault, to the point that more students came to ask me for consultations. They also took the model and tried it themselves."

SAVI analysis.
Students (figure 16): Fighting—"yelling and screaming at each other"—Square 1

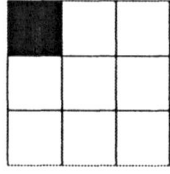

Figure 16

Teacher:
Pre-training (figure 17): Mind reading, Proposal that they "solve their problem."—Squares 2 and 6

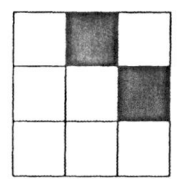

Figure 17

Post-training (figure 18): Taught and modeled conflict resolution steps for the students.
First, she gave clear instructions to the students about what they were expected to do.—Squares 5 and 6

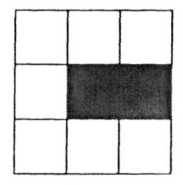

Figure 18

She instructed them each to use "I" statements—Squares 4 and 7 (figure 19).

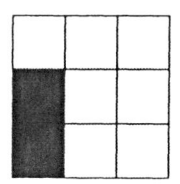

Figure 19

As they talked, she paraphrased, Square 8, and asked clarifying questions for facts—Square 5 (figure 20).

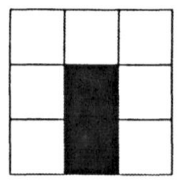

Figure 20

She then checked to see if the speaker felt heard accurately—Square 7 (figure 21).

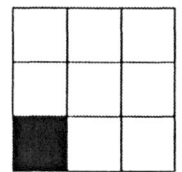

Figure 21

Results: Students learned that they were not hearing accurately, and that what they thought they were hearing was making them mad. They reported that they felt "no one was wrong."

Generalized results: Other students with conflicts came to the teacher for help with conflicts and they also took the model and tried it themselves.

Report #5: Teacher of Older Children

"I had explained to the 7th grade class that certain words such as "crap" are not appropriate for the classroom. Sometime later a student said "crap," and I asked him to rephrase his statement so that he could still show frustration. A second student piped up, "Did he say 'crap'?" At an earlier time in my career, I would have taken him aside and attacked with something like, "I told you not to use the word. You used the word. And now you have lunch detention." I took him aside and I shared my inner experience that I took it personally when he disrespected my laying down the rules. This was effective. He didn't use "crap" again. Developmentally I am at the place where I get benefit from using SAVI in retrospect more than being able to use it in the present. In this case, I could identify where I was in the SAVI grid (and where I might have been!) and notice how effective my communication had been. SAVI gave me a framework for understanding why it went so well and why successful communication was not a surprise."

SAVI Analysis.
Student: expresses inappropriate verbal behavior.

Teacher:
Pre-training (figure 22): Attack through voice tone "I told you not to do it." Punishment of student: "you have detention"—Square 1

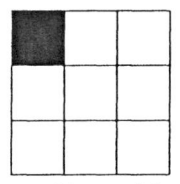

Figure 22

Post-training (figure 23): Shares inner experience—Square 7

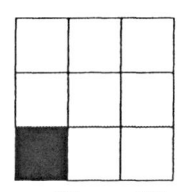

Figure 23

Results: Student does not repeat inappropriate behavior.

Report #6: Teacher of Older Children

"A parent was upset and had a conference with me because her son had been suspended from school after several incidents, and we hadn't communicated with her that he would be suspended if the behavior continued. After she spoke to me, I consciously summarized what she was saying, I noted her concern, and her wishes in terms of better communication. It was very instructive to me that through this approach I didn't get defensive (I didn't Yes-but or Discount her feelings about what had occurred with her son). I noted immediately that this communication approach calmed her. Then I was able to explain why the school made the decision that we made."

SAVI analysis.
Situation: Parent is "upset" with teacher and school.

Teacher:
Pre-training (figure 24): Self-defense (explanations about why what was done was done, Discount parents feelings by Yes-buts and data about why parent shouldn't feel that way)—Squares 1 and 3

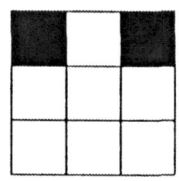

Figure 24

Post-training (figure 25): Consciously Summarized parent's position, Mirrored parent's feelings, acknowledged the parent's desire for better communication from the school.—Squares 7 and 8

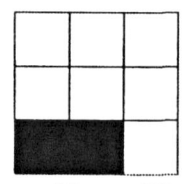

Figure 25

Results: Parent "calmed down" and could then better take in data about the school's decision.

Report #7: Teacher of Younger Children, Reflecting on Her Discoveries About the Impact of SAVI for Her in Several Roles: Interacting with Students, Interacting with Peers and Interacting with her Family

"On the first tier of exposure to SAVI, it was hard not to think that the SAVI grid was not value-laden. There is a reality that we all want to be doing more Green

Light communications than Red Light; however there is a tendency to be judgmental as a result. In our workshop group, we got pretty quickly to the second tier, seeing SAVI as a way to describe communication. So I could just notice what was going on without becoming judgmental.

Since that first workshop, I've carried the SAVI grid around with me in my wallet. I don't understand the entire grid, I don't even know what all the labels mean, and that's fine. I am still interested in it and I expect I will flesh it out.

I feel like my mothering, my role as a wife, being with a partner and communicating has been strongly influenced by SAVI. I've had a lot of insights identifying what I do and what I draw on, what my partner does, and what my kids do. It helps define what is going on. Then I have more choice in my reactions. I've taken it on as my responsibility to control what I do. By taking responsibility for the communications with my family, there have been major dynamic shifts. For instance, through SAVI, I noticed that I had a different way of communicating at home and at school. And here was a central clearing system for reducing noise. Part of it is that the parent role is different from the teacher role. I noticed that my communication style at home included mind reads, negative predictions, leading questions, and "oughtitudes." I found that by importing the techniques I used at school (especially agreements, paraphrases, and builds), I got better results at home. In that sense I have slightly professionalized my home communication environment, and things are now are much better.

I've had a lot of self-discovery. I've definitely been able to see when I make a lot of noise in my communications. With the kids at school, I ask students to report on their Surprises, Learnings, Discoveries, Satisfactions, and Dissatisfactions. I get really great open-ended answers from those five open ended questions that tend to evoke Green Light communication.

Right away, after the workshop, some other things popped right out at me, like problematic communications on the job such as gossip and joking around. SAVI provided a way of understanding why sometimes jokes work and sometimes they don't. I don't just let jokes slip by now. Another example was that the whole group of teachers suddenly was aware when we were interrupting. So I learned that I would be blocking the goal of the group communication by interrupting.

Here is an interesting fact. Part of the group of teachers thinks there is a SAVI cult. There's always that danger with something new, that someone will see it as bigger than it is. I found SAVI a really good tool. It's like when you buy a curriculum. You don't have to invent it. I don't know whether it's the complete curriculum, but it's a lot better than I could do on my own.

Red Light communication mucks up the communication so that you don't stay on message. You could get distracted from the point (for example, that a child needs to make amends for a harmful action) by getting drawn into a fight with the child. So much of my thinking about my own communication is that my Green Light communications keep me on message."

SAVI analysis. This teacher is generalizing about interactions with others across several areas of her life. Her process of "knowing the grid but not really knowing it" is a common, and we think necessary, step in shifting from a total focus on content (what is being talked about) to being able to focus both on the content, but also on process (how things are being said, that is, what behaviors are being used to say it). She reports insights about the effect of noise (Red Light behaviors, specifically Interruptions, Gossip, Joking around) on work settings, and how these behaviors negatively affect productivity and morale—Joking Around can mask real issues "as if" they weren't important. She also notes that arguing with a student (e.g., "You're wrong," "I'm not," "Yes you are," "No I'm not!") can distract from the real lesson that the teacher is trying to convey.

Analysis

The seven teachers who contributed the anecdotes above reported that SAVI helped them understand what behaviors enabled them to move toward their goal of managing discipline situations more effectively. The following summarizes the behaviors these teachers reported using:

- gives Facts
- asks Fact Questions
- asks Broad Questions
- Proposals
- asks Feeling Questions
- Mirrors Feelings
- Paraphrases
- Summarizes
- Tells own Feelings
- Mirrors Feelings

Red, Yellow, Green 123

They also reported that they thought that without having SAVI as a map they would have been more likely to use Attacks, Blame, Mind Reads, Gossip, Joking Around, Leading Questions, Yes-Buts, Discounts, Oughtitudes, Interruptions, Opinions and Proposals.

We saw in the SAVI analysis of each teacher's report that these different sets of behaviors made very different patterns in the SAVI Grid, with different potentials for information transfer. We have summarized below the behaviors teachers reported using pre-workshop (figure 26) and post-workshop (figure 27).

Figure 26

Teacher Reports of Likely Pre-workshop Behaviors in Conflictual Situations

1 Attacks Blames	2 Mind Reads Gossip Joking Around	3 Leading Questions Yes-buts Discounts Oughtitudes Interrupts
4	5	6 Opinions Proposals
7	8	9

Figure 27
Teacher Reports of Actual Post-workshop Behaviors in Conflictual Situations

1	2	3
4	5 Gives Facts Asks Fact Questions Asks Broad Questions	6 Proposals
7 Asks Feeling Questions Mirrors Feelings	8 Paraphrases Summarizes	9

To someone overhearing a conversation conducted in the pre-workshop behaviors, the discussion would sound like a competition or a fight. If you want to experiment with this yourself, try to make a joint decision with someone just using the behaviors in Squares 1, 2, 3 and 6!

After training, the behaviors teachers used formed a pattern that demonstrates that information is getting processed: Facts are given to support conclusions, information is Paraphrased and Summarized, Questions are asked directly, feelings are expressed and accepted by Mirroring.

The SAVI map allowed teachers to focus on the shift from Opinion to Fact, from Attack to Paraphrase or restatement, from "shoulds" (Opinions and Oughtitudes) to Questions, etc. In the above anecdotal reports, these communication shifts made a significant difference in how teachers and students experienced resolution of the types of problems commonly thought of as "discipline problems."

Examples of strategies that teachers modeled in their post-workshop behaviors were:

- If student is in Red light, don't join in Red light.
- If student is discounting what you say, often it is because they have misheard or are misunderstanding what you are saying. Use behaviors which get you heard, for example, repeat the facts: "These are the directions for your project." Ask student to repeat the facts: "What did you understand me to say?"
- If students are fighting, act like a behavioral "filter". Filter out the Red Light behavior, and transmit their information back and forth between them using Green Light behavior. For example, "George, this is what I heard you say.... Is that what you said? Paul, this is what I heard you say.... Is that what you said?"

The pattern of changes that these teachers report parallels what would be predicted from Agazarian's theory. She used an adaptation of Kurt Lewin's (1951) force field model to map the driving and restraining forces to effective information transfer (Agazarian, 1986) (see Figure 28).

Figure 28

Force Field Influencing Boundary Permeability to Communication	
Driving Forces	Restraining Forces
Asking Direct Questions →	← Indirect Questions ← Leading Questions ← Sarcastic Questions
Answering Questions →	← Avoiding Answering ← Changing the Subject ← Answering a Question with a Question
Building on Ideas → Proposing → Owning Own Feelings → Supporting Self and Others →	← Pre-empting Ideas ← Yes-butting ← Interrupting ← Blaming and Complaining ← Putting Self Down ← Oughts and Shoulds

From Agazarian (1987) p. 3

As an extension of these ideas, the head of the school has reported his impression that as people create and use the SAVI-based strategies, these new behaviors evolve into new roles that move school culture toward its educational goals.

Summary

This chapter tracked the impact of SAVI—a tool that can be used for monitoring communication process—in an elementary school setting two years after its introduction. We focused on teachers' reports of their behavior, particularly how they talked when there was conflict. Anecdotal staff reports illustrating the types of changes made in classroom communication were cited.

We illustrated an example of how using an observation system like SAVI turns any single "event" in the classroom into data for action research. Teachers, administrators and parents can see whether their behaviors are actually supporting their educational goals, or moving away from them. They can, on a case-by-case basis, do research by collecting and analyzing the data about which behaviors make what differences.

In this school, the introduction of the tool was used in situations of conflict to encourage the teachers to objectively describe what the student said, what the teacher said and what happened subsequently by using Facts (Square 5, the central square of the SAVIGrid).

SAVI gave teachers a frame within which they could be deliberate about choosing their behavior, and to see whether their choices were effective or not. These resources in turn helped the teachers shift out of personal reactions and into a research mode—identifying behaviors that supported their goals.

We look forward to further interactions with the staff of this school, and others, to continue to pilot the effects of familiarity with SAVI in reducing restraining forces and increasing driving forces toward the schools' goals.

7

Functional Subgrouping in the Classroom: A Powerful Tool for Learning

Irene McHenry, Ph.D., Friends Council on Education

This chapter details my investigation of the use of functional subgrouping in a school context. I introduced the systems-centered training (SCT) method of functional subgrouping in four different age-level classrooms as a technique for dialogue with the goal of facilitating learning through the process of joining on similarities rather than separating on differences during class discussion. A secondary goal was to improve my skills in facilitating the functional subgrouping technique and to find effective ways to teach and use functional subgrouping in school environments. The findings from my investigation suggest that functional subgrouping is an effective dialogue method for deepening student understanding of academic content, for engaging students at an emotional level to enhance their cognitive learning, for engaging students in a meta-cognitive process during a class discussion and for developing listening skills.

Having studied systems-centered theory and practiced the technique of functional subgrouping in experiential training groups, I was curious about the adaptability of functional subgrouping for use in the academic classroom. Common practices for academic class discussion include debate, critique and responses to the teacher's questions toward the goal of critical thinking. I undertook to satisfy my curiosity about the learning that might come from functional subgrouping by designing an investigation in which I introduced the practice of functional subgrouping to students of various ages in four different academic classrooms. My goals were to learn about the use of functional subgrouping in an educational setting and to improve both my teaching about the subgrouping technique and my facilitation of classroom discussions using functional subgrouping.

This investigation was designed using an inquiry approach grounded in the methodology of action research in education. Action research in an educational context empowers the teacher as a researcher in the classroom in direct relationship with the students as active, contributing participants in the inquiry (Sagor, 1991). Action research includes first-person self-observation of the teacher's actions. This self-observation in my study was used to inform, amend, and possibly transform my own leadership interventions as a teacher. The participatory aspect of the investigation included a second-person collaborative inquiry, which had the capacity to influence the group's performance (Reason & Bradbury, 2000). My collaboration with the students had two parts: 1) the class was invited to participate by using the functional subgrouping method for their discussion, and 2) the class members were invited to participate in a reflection on their learning and the use of the functional subgrouping method. This group reflection generated data for my reflection as a researcher.

The Design of the Study

In my role as class teacher, I introduced functional subgrouping to four different student groups in two different educational institutions:

- Two different classes of a graduate level course on ethics with 25 adult students in each class;
- One class of nine high school juniors and seniors in an elective course on comparative world religions in a private high school;
- One class of 20 seventh grade students in a required course on religion and values in a private school.

For each group, I gathered information from the students after using the functional subgrouping method through a reflective group review activity, which took place immediately following the subgrouping experience. The activity used was "surprises, learnings, satisfactions, dissatisfactions, and discoveries" (Agazarian, 1997, p. 72). An analysis of these student responses after each class session generated action steps for further refinement of how and when to use the functional subgrouping method to facilitate learning.

The findings from this investigation are described below for each classroom experience. I describe each experience as a cycle of my own learning about the use of functional subgrouping in the classroom. For each cycle described, there is a brief description of the students, a brief description of what I did as the teacher to introduce functional subgrouping, a summary of the students' reflections on their experience, and a summary of my own learning.

Learning Cycle 1—Graduate Course on Ethics

The students were 25 adult students in a graduate level course on ethics. The classroom discussion topic centered on three articles on Buddhism and the concept of desire. The students had read the articles outside of class. My goal was to use functional subgrouping to generate a spontaneous student-centered discussion within the class, rather than to have students respond to teacher-directed questions.

I introduced the functional subgrouping technique to the class during the first 10 minutes of class in the following way:

- I described functional subgrouping as a technique for deepening our learning from discussion by having class members join the discussion when they felt a level of resonance or similarity with the perspective being discussed.
- I drew a diagram on the board using one large circle to represent the whole class with three small circles within to represent the different subgroups that might develop during the discussion.
- I emphasized the importance of each class member joining the discussion when someone felt a resonance or similarity with the previous speaker.
- I gave examples of how to join on similarities.
- I gave examples of pseudo joining, as in "yes, butting" (Agazarian, 1996).
- I talked about the idea of joining on similarities first, and then later discriminating the subtle differences within the similar subgroup.
- I emphasized the importance of careful listening.
- I gave them a ground rule of letting one subgroup develop itself before another one started.

The question posed for the discussion was:
What was your experience of learning from reading these articles?

In facilitating functional subgrouping, I made simple interventions to keep students on track with the method, especially noting when someone brought in a different perspective, as if they were joining a subgroup that was already exploring their responses to a concept from the reading. Each time, I would ask the student to hold the difference until the working group was finished with their exploration. In the group reflection following the discussion, three major themes emerged: the challenge of using the functional subgrouping technique; the strong emotional engagement in the discussion as a result of using the functional subgrouping method; and a sense of deeper listening to each other and coming to new understandings from the use of the functional subgrouping technique.

The following excerpts from the group reflection illustrate these themes.

The Challenge:

"It was difficult and dissatisfying to stay quiet while a different subgroup worked."
"It was difficult and dissatisfying to stay in one subgroup."
"I was dissatisfied that I had a hard time figuring out how to join in the discussion."
"I was surprised that I wanted to listen to everyone and I couldn't decide who to join."
"It was surprised that it sounded so simple, yet it was really hard to do."

Emotional engagement:

"I was surprised that I had strong feelings while listening."
"I'm surprised that it felt like we were having fun, while it was a serious discussion."
"I'm very satisfied that I felt so inspired by the discussion."
"I discovered that I could feel really fired up."

Deeper listening and learning:

"I'm satisfied that I felt listened to."
"I'm surprised that the discussion went into a direction we didn't anticipate—we learned something!"
"I'm surprised that many of us had much more to say after the discussion ended."
"Yes, we just wanted to keep talking."
"I was surprised that I had more to say than I usually do in class, maybe because I was really listening to what everyone else had to say."

As the teacher, I decided to make the following adjustments for the next class: 1) Develop a detailed handout of guidelines for functional subgrouping to reduce the initial anxiety and sense of difficulty about using this technique.
2) Use an assignment for the next cycle that lends itself to engaging the emotional level, rather than a didactic, intellectual topic.
3) Carefully construct the discussion topic so that it is a question about present experience, in order to further support emotional engagement.

Learning Cycle 2—A Second Graduate Course on Ethics

The students were 25 adult students in different (from Cycle 1) graduate level course on ethics. This time, I introduced the technique of functional subgrouping during the first 10 minutes of class by giving students a handout that described guidelines for functional subgrouping. Each item on the handout was reviewed and clarified as students asked questions. The items were:

- Functional subgrouping is a technique for new and deepened learning from a class discussion.
- Different subgroups will develop during the discussion.
- Let one subgroup develop itself fully before starting a different one (This is not our usual norm).
- It is important for each class member to join the discussion when feeling a real resonance or similarity with the previous speaker. (Examples)
- Beware of pseudo joining, as in "yes, butting." (Examples)
- Join on similarities first, and then later discriminate the subtle differences within the similar subgroup.
- Very careful listening is required.

Functional subgrouping was used for a class discussion following the class activity of students reading aloud from their autobiographical "Values" papers. After the highlights from the papers were shared, I introduced the discussion topic: Talk about your present experience after hearing the excerpts from the values papers.

Students frequently referred to their handout while participating in the discussion. The handout was a useful tool for self-correction; students noticed and stopped themselves when they were in the middle of joining with a difference and waited for their turn to start a new subgroup. In the group reflection following the discussion, students spoke about how the use of the functional subgrouping technique engaged them strongly at an emotional level, increasing their learning and understanding:

> "I discovered that the discussion deepened my understanding of my family and how they influenced my values."
> "I'm surprised that I had a new understanding of how fathers feel about their children."
> "I discovered a feeling of forgiveness for my absent father."

"I was inspired to learn from the depth of the discussion that men can be sensitive and compassionate."

"I'm feeling very satisfied to discover that most people found role models for their values in their families."

"I learned that we have to let go of the hate and frustration from the past, take a realistic view of the present, and now look toward how to make the future better."

"I'm surprised that I feel free of hatred, as a result of this discussion."

During Learning Cycle 2, I observed that students were less frustrated by the practice of functional subgrouping and were able to use the technique quickly and easily. This group's training about functional subgrouping was more direct and clear because they had the use of the written guidelines. Given that it is a norm in the academic classroom for the teacher to provide handouts, students may have felt more confident in the use of the technique with the written guide in their hands for reference during the discussion. I observed that the students were careful in helping each other to use the functional subgrouping technique effectively. Students were able to give space to the students who were working in subgroups, and all students were really listening to each other. A second observation during Learning Cycle 2 was that the discussion was rich and filled with feeling. Some students were moved to tears during the discussion. Some students embraced each other after the discussion.

My learning from this experience confirmed the systems-centered theory related to the practice of functional subgrouping. The functional subgrouping method provided a structure that focused the students' energy toward the goal of listening in order to communicate, increased the clarity and depth of the communication, and set a climate for exploring the complexity of perspectives and emotions. Choosing a discussion topic that focused everyone's awareness to the present apprehensive and comprehensive experience engaged the emotional level as well as the cognitive and facilitated the functional use of functional subgrouping in this academic classroom.

Learning Cycle 3—High School Students

For this cycle, I decided to try functional subgrouping with a class of nine juniors and seniors in high school in a private school in an elective course in comparative world religions. My intention was to introduce functional subgrouping as briefly as possible without a paper handout of guidelines that might be perceived as "rules" and be met with normal adolescent resistance. I introduced functional subgrouping with a brief description, exactly as I had done for Cycle 1. The stu-

dents had read and discussed Herman Hess's novel *Siddhartha*, and they had written journal responses to each chapter with the goal of relating their own life experience to that of Siddhartha in the novel. The functional subgrouping technique was introduced for the final class discussion of the novel, and the discussion question was:
What was your experience of the novel Siddhartha?

These students had difficulty using the functional subgrouping technique. They rarely made eye contact with each other; they kept looking toward me, and I redirected them to look at the person they were joining with. Several times, students burst into laughter while trying to hold eye contact during the discussion. I wondered if the self-consciousness of the adolescent stage of development and the small size of this group were factors making eye contact difficult.

During the group reflection after the discussion, only two of the nine students expressed positive learning outcomes from the subgrouping experience. I believe that these reflections were honest and profound for this group:

> "I learned that it felt good for us to talk to each other instead of to the teacher."
> "I learned that it would be good if we could talk like this to each other more, then we might take each other's ideas more seriously in real life."

All of the students expressed a feeling of resistance to the idea of joining on similarities, and waiting to bring in differences. Even though I had tried to avoid introducing subgrouping with a set of "rules," the implicit structure of the functional subgrouping technique felt like rules to these adolescents, as the following comments illustrate.

> "I was very dissatisfied because I felt 'trapped' by the rule of building with one group before going against someone's idea."
> "I learned that I like being able to disagree with someone right away without waiting, which is the way we usually do it in class."
> "I was dissatisfied because I think a discussion works better when you can disagree immediately with what someone says and you don't have to wait."
> "I was surprised that the same people who usually have a lot to say talked more in this discussion and the ones who are usually quiet didn't talk in this discussion either."

In reflecting on cycle 3, I realized that it was a mistake not to use a written handout outlining the guidelines for functional subgrouping. A written handout, like the one I used with the college class, could have reduced the students' anxiety about the method, and it would have given me the opportunity to encourage them to curiously experiment with this new process, thus reducing the idea that the activity was about following rules. I decided to see if written guidelines, using an age-appropriate metaphor, and using language to engage their curiosity about experimenting with something new, would be effective for younger adolescents.

Learning Cycle 4—Seventh Grade

For cycle 4, I had the opportunity to introduce the functional subgrouping technique for dialogue to 20 students in the 7th grade in a required course on religion and values in a private school. The discussion in which functional subgrouping was used followed a homework assignment in which the students read a chapter about the life and vision of William Penn and wrote a response to a question; I used the this same question as the class discussion topic:
Based on your experience and your reading, was Penn's Holy Experiment (the founding of Pennsylvania) a success or a failure? Why?

In order to encourage exploration and curiosity, I used the metaphor of "exploration teams" to introduce functional subgrouping without using the word "subgrouping". I told the students we were trying out a new way to explore the vast territory around a question in which there was no right or wrong answer. I wrote guidelines for functional subgrouping in 7th grade language called "Exploring the Territory." The guidelines (Appendix 1) talked about forming exploration teams. The guidelines included a discussion about "eye energy" as a way to stay connected within exploration teams and "deep listening with curiosity" to other exploration teams who were exploring different territory. I continually used the exploration team metaphor and the concept of maintaining curiosity throughout the 10-minute introduction to the technique and throughout the facilitation of the discussion.

These 7th graders, to my surprise, used the functional subgrouping technique very well. By the end of the 30-minute discussion, students were monitoring themselves and reminding each other to listen when another exploration team was working. Students consistently and actively stated which team they were joining when adding a thought or feeling to the discussion. All students actively participated in the discussion, and some were able to describe new learning and follow the discussion at a meta-cognitive level, as the following reflective comments illustrate:

> "I was surprised that three people actually thought the colony was a failure."
> "I was surprised that most people were in the 'undecided' subgroup."

Functional Subgrouping in the Classroom: A Powerful Tool for Learning

> "I was surprised that two new topics came up and were discussed: racism and capital punishment. They seemed to be off the topic, yet there were part of exploring the territory of the topic."

The students showed evidence of deep listening and learning about both process and content from the discussion, as is shown from the following comments:

> "I learned that all opinions were right in a certain way."
> "I was satisfied that not everyone went into the undecided group."
> "I was satisfied that I didn't take things personally when someone had a different opinion than mine."
> "Listening to the other points of view while they built up was satisfying to me."

This group of adolescent students described the challenge of using functional subgrouping in ways similar to the descriptions of the older adolescents. Their main challenge was in restraining the impulse to speak up immediately in disagreement with a speaker. These students, like the older adolescents, said they preferred to argue and debate rather than use the functional subgrouping technique, even though they were very aware of their deep learning from the use of the technique.

> "I had a hard time staying with my team. I wanted to say something about each team's ideas."
> "I was dissatisfied that I was not allowed to debate and I wanted to debate." (5 out of 20 students had this same response, worded slightly differently).
> "I couldn't keep up with the argument. When I had to wait for my group, I forgot what I wanted to say."
> "I didn't like it that we couldn't argue. I think more points would have come out, if we could have argued."
> "I was dissatisfied that the time was short. I only got to talk once."

In reflecting on cycle 4, I was pleased with the success the 7th graders experienced in the use of the functional subgrouping technique. I observed that the "exploration team" metaphor worked very well for these young adolescents and may be useful with older adolescents. Finding the appropriate metaphor for the age level and interest level of this group was very valuable in order to describe the functional subgrouping process in a way that was easily understood and used by the group. Giving the written guidelines and age-appropriate terms such as "eye energy" also facilitated their capacity to subgroup.

I observed that the students with longer attention spans and higher-level abstract thinking skills were able to use functional subgrouping better than the other students. I discovered that some 7th grade students have a well-developed capacity for meta-cognitive observations during group process. I observed that some 7th grade students have the capacity to contain their point of view while listening intently to others. For others, this is a difficult task.

I learned that arguing is the preferred discussion habit for most of these 7th graders. I believe that their ability to express their desire to argue within the framework of a dissatisfaction provided the opportunity for increased awareness of the impulse to argue, and therefore, over time, might help them to contain the impulse, as they had done so successfully in this discussion. It is also important to note, given the expressed dissatisfaction about not arguing, that the next day in class, many students asked with enthusiasm, if we were going to "do exploration teams again." Over the course of the term, students preferred the "exploration team" method for any class discussion.

Summary and Recommendations

A summary of these four cycles of thinking, acting, and reflecting on the use of functional subgrouping indicates that functional subgrouping is an effective technique for dialogue in school classrooms. Functional subgrouping keeps the class task-focused; provides a method for exploring a perspective deeply before moving on in the discussion; requires good listening behavior from the students; provides a way for students to contain (hold) their differences knowing that they will have a time to explore these differences; engages students in emotional learning by keeping boundaries open to different perspectives and by staying engaged in the energy of the group; and provides a structure for clarity of communication (as ambiguity is reduced by the requirement of joining a subgroup and building with a similarity).

Specific considerations for the teacher, which come from my investigation, are:

- Develop a group-specific, age-appropriate metaphor and related language to introduce the functional subgrouping concept and process.
- Create a simple handout of guidelines appropriate to the group using the appropriate metaphor.
- Frame the goal of functional subgrouping as a learning goal. This emphasizes functional subgrouping as an appropriate tool for educators and students in a learning environment.

- Focus on students' natural curiosity about the use of functional subgrouping, which is a driving force toward using the technique.
- Highlight the meta-cognitive task for the group by introducing functional subgrouping as an experiment for class discussion and invite the group to pay attention to what they are learning while using the technique.
- Carefully construct the wording of the discussion topic, so that it asks a question about present experience, thus allowing for emotional engagement on resonances when using academic content material.
- Provide ample time at the end of the group dialogue for reflecting on the experience. Use the "Surprises and Learnings" activity to structure this reflection. A force field activity (Agazarian, 1997) could also be used for reflection on the learning.

As the teacher, I found that participation in an ongoing, experiential systems-centered training (SCT) group was essential for building my skills in implementing functional subgrouping in the classroom. I strongly recommend ongoing training in SCT for teachers who wish to implement functional subgrouping in their classrooms.

Contribution to the Field of Education

The renowned founder of the progressive and experiential education movements, John Dewey first legitimized the practice of examining one's own experience as a source of knowledge. He advocated teaching and learning based on action and reflective activity. "Dewey's (1938) discourse on reflective thinking was very influential on Lewin (1946) and his development of the action research method, as well as on the 'teacher as researcher' movement in education" (Witt, 1998, p.8). The use of functional subgrouping as a method for class discussion legitimizes experiential knowing in combination with academic content in a way that can be transformative for the learner, as shown in this investigation.

An important discovery from this investigation is that functional subgrouping around a particular content-area assignment engages the emotional aspect of learning, not just the intellectual. Through functional subgrouping, both apprehensive knowing and comprehensive knowing are accessed and engaged as the participants resonate to the similarity of a working subgroup and bring their experiences and insights into the discussion. This dynamic aspect of class discussion via functional subgrouping is worth further investigation as it relates to learning theory and current research on emotional intelligence and the multiple intelligences (Gardner, 1999; Goleman, 1998).

For further research, a next step would be to design a participatory action research study in which functional subgrouping is introduced at the beginning of a course as the primary method for class discussion throughout the semester. Using the functional subgrouping method consistently throughout the course will provide regular opportunities for the same group of students to practice and increase their capacity to use the technique over time and to strengthen their listening skills and their capacity to discern (emotionally and cognitively) similarities and differences in perspective and understanding. A working hypothesis is that the class would also build a sense of trust that will facilitate the exploration of academic content at deeper levels by giving students a structure to discriminate and integrate differences in perception and understanding. At the end of the course, it would be possible to evaluate how the practice of functional subgrouping enlivens dialogue while stimulating insight and understanding, and how the consistent use of the functional subgrouping technique affects the group process and phases of group development of the class. The results of such evaluations would provide more information about how functional subgrouping might contribute to transformational learning.

Appendix 1—Exploration Teams

Goal: to explore an issue in a way that

- allows us to learn something new by listening deeply to others,
- allows us to explore all of the different thoughts and feelings about an issue,
- deepens our understanding of the issue,
- generates creative thinking and problem-solving about the issue.

How to do the exploration:
- Everyone's job is LISTENING—exquisite, careful, <u>curious</u> listening.
- Each person's job is to <u>join</u> an exploration team to explore the territory of a certain thought or feeling.

Creating the first exploration team:
1. The discussion begins when one person states a thought/feeling on the issue.
2. Reflect on that response to see if you have a SIMILAR thought or feeling.
3. If you can JOIN the person who first spoke, then tell her/him your thoughts or feelings that are similar.

> To say, "I agree" or "I feel the same way" is NOT joining.
> To say, "Yes, but" is NOT joining.
> Joining is done by describing your thought or feeling in detail. This adds more information and understanding of the territory.

4. Use your "eye energy" to stay in contact with others on your exploration team, especially while a different team is exploring a different territory of the issue.
5. If you are not joining the present exploration, listen with respect and curiosity.

Creating the second exploration team:
6. After the 1st team has had a chance to explore similar territory, someone may introduce a very different thought or feeling as a "difference."
7. If you have a similar response to this "difference", then JOIN by telling your thoughts or feelings that are similar.
8. During the time that the second team is forming, the first team listens with respect and curiosity. The first team stays connected in silence through eye energy.

Creating additional teams:
9. There may be additional teams, even a team who explores the territory of "not knowing what I think/feel about the issue right now."

At the end of the discussion, we will share our surprises, learnings, satisfactions, dissatisfactions and discoveries with each other.

8

Meetings that Work: Making Common Sense "Common"

Beulah Trey, Ph.D., Center for Applied Research
Susan P. Gantt, Ph.D., CGP, ABPP, Emory University School of Medicine
Claude Marchessault, MA, Strategic Leadership

Everyone has experienced dissatisfaction with meetings either as the leader or an attendee. This article uses systems-centered training (SCT) to explain some typical problems with meetings and offers practical solutions to optimize the flow of information into and out of the meeting. By shifting perspectives from an individual-oriented to a systems-oriented perspective, group members can begin to give constructive feedback to the meeting system without assigning blame to individuals. The process that emerges out of this perspective helps to decrease personalization in meetings and builds a system of meetings that creates the best possible climate for getting work done. The authors split meetings into three distinct yet inseparable parts: the beginning, middle, and end. The goal of the beginning of the meeting is to assign leadership roles and get everyone into the "member role." The middle of the meeting is the time when work gets done and when leaders keep tabs on the process by which the group is doing work. The end of the meeting is designed to increase the likelihood that the group's work will continue through identifying next steps and allows the refinement of the meeting process by reviewing how the meeting went.

Each week in organizations across the country, leaders get together with their staff, often prepared with clear objectives, good meeting structures, facilitation skills and pre-posted agendas. Yet more often than they'd like, staff leave these weekly meetings thinking but not saying, "What a waste of time! If I say anything in there, I'll get attacked or they'll just take it over. Besides, any important decision is made outside the meeting anyway. And the meeting will only drag on longer while we go over same stuff we went over before." And the leaders leave wondering, "Why aren't people saying what they think? Don't they care what happens to this organization? What a waste of talent!" Add to this frustration and ineffectiveness the collective salaries and travel expenses represented around the table and these kinds of poor results come at a very high premium to the organization. Yet meetings, whether formal or informal, are a central activity critical to the success of any organizations, (Oppenheim, 1987). They are the essential points of contact between positions and departments, departments and work groups, between strategies and values. They are the important forums where information is exchanged and decisions are made that move the organization forward. When meetings work, knowledge is shared, common goals are re-affirmed, buy-in is established, and group identity and team and organizational interaction are achieved.

This article is about how to produce engaging and productive meetings *deliberately and consistently* by applying systems-centered training (SCT). The theory and methods of SCT highlight the invisible, and often missed, key success factor in meetings—the system. It is by addressing meetings as a system, that we area able to transform them into compelling, effective and fun activities, where good decisions are made, innovative ideas are generated, information is shared, organizational energy is increased, synergies are developed, and alignment to common goals achieved.

System-centered training teaches us to see the system, not just the people. This shift in focus challenges many of the conventional ways we've learned to perceive and manage meetings. Yet it is seeing and working with the "system" of a meeting that is at the heart of what allows us to get the informed and engaging results we all want from our meetings.

To begin to understand how to manage a system, let's first be clear about what a system is. Though much simpler than a living human system, a car is a helpful example of a system. It is a *mechanical* system that requires fuel, a tank to put the fuel in, an engine to convert the fuel from gas to movement, and a steering mechanism to direct where it is going. And above all, for the car to actually go anywhere, it requires a person to drive it!

Living human systems are both similar and different from cars. The similarities are that a living human system requires energy (the fuel in a car), a boundary that contains the energy (the fuel tank), a way to manage the human differences so they are integrated and the system transforms (the engine turns gas into movement), and a mechanism for directing its transformed energy towards its goal (the driver). Unlike cars, however, living human systems are emergent rather than mechanical. This essential difference is at the heart of living human systems. In fact, every living human system can be described in terms of how the system organizes information [the energy in living human systems (Miller, 1978)], how it orients to its goals and how it self-corrects (Agazarian, 1997). The challenging difference here is that living human systems are changing and developing themselves simultaneous as they do their work.

Why Bother to Think Systems?

Applying systems-centered thinking and methods to help us see a meeting as a living human system offers two important advantages:

1. Seeing the system and not just the people decreases personalizing and the all too frequent "emotional hijacking" that it triggers. "Personalizing" describes the process by which group members see an event or action as being characteristic of a person while also not seeing the context and meaning that are not related to the person. For example, when you label someone as careless as they trip over an uneven sidewalk, you are personalizing the event that may have as much to do with the uneven sidewalk, the person's frame of mind, and/or companions as the person's lack of coordination at that moment. In fact, determining the variables that caused the person to trip, that are not personal would lead to fixing the sidewalk. Staying focused on the person's carelessness allows the sidewalk to remain uneven.

When a system has less personalizing, it is always easier for the system (and the people in it) to function. The usefulness of the distinction between people and systems is highlighted in a scenario where senior executives meet to review the coming year's forecasts for a large national insurance company. It starts when Tom, the CFO, raises a question about the accuracy of the data. Immediately, many of his colleagues at the table find themselves rolling their eyes and thinking, "There goes Tom again, doing his usually worrying thing. How many times do we have to go through this?" Donna, the Senior VP for Strategic Planning, takes Tom's concerns as an attack on her ability to provide the team with accurate data and quickly steps in to defend the data—and her self. Tom's concern is quickly reframed as being "characteristic" of Tom. Sensing Donna's vulnerability, the team accepts Donna's generalized reassurance, dodges the personality reference to Tom, and abruptly moves on to another topic of discussion. Little time is taken to find out about Tom's concerns or to see if anyone else shares them, never mind determining their validity. The group may have missed an important flaw in the data as a result.

Taking a system's perspective, in this case, shifts our attention away from the people and their personal reactions—Tom, Donna or the team's—and instead focuses it on tracking how the team explores a concern when it is raised. In the example, the team reacted to the people and failed to assess the merit of the information and, as a consequence, the team's decision-making suffered and the meeting itself was de-energized.

2. The other advantage to a systems perspective is that describing the system properties of a meeting makes it possible to replicate those aspects of the meeting that work, while identifying those aspects that can be improved—independently of the particular people who helped it work well or poorly. This makes it easier for a team or work group to continue functioning at a high level in the face of personnel changes, for example. Absent an understanding of the system norms that support the meeting's productivity, we are commonly focused on attributions of the leader or key people to try to account for meeting failure or success.

Seeing a Meeting as a System

Running effective meetings using systems-centered thinking means monitoring four specific areas:

1. How does information (the fuel for living human systems) come into the meeting?
2. How does talk (the major vehicle for delivering information in a meeting) get filtered to take the noise out?
3. How do decisions get made and conflicts and differences get used as resources rather than being divisive?
4. How does the system keep itself on track or get back on track when it gets lost?

1. How Does Information (the Fuel for Living Human Systems) Come Into the Meeting?

SCT borrows from Miller's (1978) introduction to living systems and equates energy in living human systems with information. Without information, the energy that fuels living humans systems, the system will literally be unable to work. All of us have had frustrating experiences where the information the team needs to do its work is missing. Our frustration is compounded when we learn that a crucial piece of information about the existence of a report was actually available, but not mentioned. Later, we learn that someone was afraid to mention it because they feared they would be blamed for the bad numbers in the report.

Thinking about system boundaries and observing when the boundaries of a system open to information and when they close to information makes it possible to look at how the system manages information flow. In closed systems, very little information comes in. In the example above, the boundaries closed when the person believed his "negative prediction" that he would be blamed. Believing this thought stopped him from bringing in relevant and important information. SCT (Agazarian & Gantt, 2003; Gantt & Agazarian, 2004) has identified speculations and negative predictions as common communications in meetings that close down the flow of information. A leader using SCT then focuses on weakening these speculations and negative predictions by changing them into hypotheses that can be tested. This shifts the orientation in a meeting toward problem solving and reality-testing. In this example, the question is asked: do people get blamed for bringing in negative information? If the answer is yes, then the system can evaluate whether this is a productive norm; if the answer is no, then the person can be encouraged to bring in the information.

SCT views information as including both facts and team members' responses to the facts. This means that team members are responsible not only for the content work of the meeting but also for the candor of their responses to the meeting. If someone starts feeling that a discussion is going around and around, SCT contends that it is that person's responsibility to raise the concerns to the team. In this way, the person stays engaged and the team can check whether in fact the perception is accurate and if it is, recalibrate how to proceed.

This kind of calibration underscores an important contribution of SCT. According to SCT, systems and reality don't necessarily go together. In fact, unless norms are deliberately set to support reality-testing, reality is not a system's greatest priority. Without training and discipline, many forces pull systems out of sync with reality. When we begin to sort through communications in meetings, we quickly discover how much of our decision-making is based on something other than reality—people make decisions because they imagine someone else wants them to, or they substitute opinions or facts when they do not have all the data, or they base their decision on an imagined future or a negative prediction (Agazarian, 1997). Harvey (1974) defines in dismaying detail how systems regularly make bad decisions that no one wanted or supported based on social niceties and the difficulty of accessing and communicating one's real reactions to events.

Through weakening negative predictions and developing norms that encourage people to voice their reactions to both the content and their reactions to the meetings themselves, SCT methods help develop a system that learns to orient and re-orient itself to reality. It is the meeting leader's job to create a setting where this kind of re-calibration is possible.

2. How Does Talk (the Major Vehicle for Delivering Information in a Meeting) Get Filtered to Take the Noise Out?

Meetings are about communicating. Building on the work of Shannon and Weaver (1964), SCT attends to the two parts of all communications: the message one wants to get across and the noise that gets in the way of the message. The three major sources of noise are ambiguity and redundancy (Shannon & Weaver, 1964) and contradiction (Simon & Agazarian, 1967). When information is presented and it lacks specificity and is vague (ambiguity), the report acts as a smokescreen and people listening lose their focus. Another familiar example is a presentation that goes over information that the team already knows (redundancy). By the time there is new information, very few people are still listening or there is no time for discussion. And when contradictions come into a meeting, one side of the message always gets lost. For example, the "Yes, but" is a highly confusing contradiction that seems to signal both agreement and disagreement but usually is a vehicle for disagreeing.

Information flow is increased to the extent that noise is diminished (Shannon & Weaver, 1964).[1] With this understanding, SCT has developed practical techniques for lowering noise in communication (see middle section of this paper).

3. How Do Decisions Get Made and How Do Conflicts and Differences Get Used as Resources Rather than Being Divisive?

SCT identifies the challenge of managing conflicts and differences so the differences can be explored as being a crucial undertaking in any meeting (Agazarian & Philibossian, 1998). All too often, when a person has a viewpoint that is different, the person may withhold their viewpoint based on the idea that it is not smart to disagree or voice a different perspective. Or alternately, as soon as a team member raises a concern others step in to refute the concern, provide reassurance, or attempt to convince the "disagreeing member" about the error in their viewpoint. Or when controversial issues are raised, the discussion devolves into a debate between the first few or the most emotionally compelling alternatives. Viewpoints are presented as opposing whether or not they are actually opposing points—and the meeting participants are asked to choose between alternatives often with little information about either side.

---

1. There is an inverse relationship between noise in the communication and the probability that information in the channel will be transferred.

SCT introduces an innovative method for resolving conflicts that also strengthens decision-making: functional subgrouping (Agazarian, 1997). Functional subgrouping provides a structure for exploring each perspective well enough so there is a high likelihood that a decision integrates the diverse perspectives (Agazarian & Philibossian, 1998; Gantt & Agazarian, 2004). These points of integration between viewpoints allow for a transformation of the team's original conception of the issues (Trey, 2002). The process by which this is done is described later in this chapter.

4. How Does the System Keep Itself on Track or Get Back on Track When it Gets Off?

SCT emphasizes the importance of goal orientation in how effective meetings work. To the extent that the goal and task of a meeting are clear and that the meeting goals are aligned to the larger context, meetings run smoothly and groups develop a great ability to notice when the work is off-goal.

The remainder of this chapter describes the practical structure and organization of SCT's approach and how the ideas described above are put into practice. Some of what we are describing may remind you of what you already know and other suggestions may be new. Regardless, we want to relate these tools for leaders and meeting participants with the goal of developing systems-centered "best practices" for meetings that attend to two important goals—getting work done and building the system itself.

Meetings: Beginnings, Middles and Ends

We have divided meetings into three inseparable components—the beginning, the middle and the end. Each component has a distinctive goal and format. In the beginning the goal is to organize the meeting system in such a way that ensures that people (who provide the energy for work) are present, ready and available to focus on the work of the meeting. The goal of the middle component is to do the work of the meeting ensuring that information is shared and explored, appropriate decisions are made, and the system continues to mature. Finally the objective at the meeting's end is to close in a way that increases the likelihood that the work will move forward and the system will learn how to maintain or increase its effectiveness. The remainder of this paper focuses on each of these system components.

The Beginning: Getting Ready to Work

Meetings set a structure for work and the way they are structured influences how the work gets done. At a simplistic level, meetings are structured around time, space, membership, roles and purposes. They happen at a given time, in a given place, with a predetermined group of participants, leadership and objectives. The clarity of these structures greatly influences the team members' ability to work. Attention to these issues is the work of the beginning of meetings.

Leadership Roles

In SCT, the leader is responsible for creating a meeting structure in which work can be accomplished. In systems language, the goal of the leader's role is to set the structure for work. This means the leader is responsible for making the meeting's time, place, membership and overarching goal known.

At the beginning of the meeting itself, the leader sets the context for the meeting. First leadership roles are identified. SCT recognizes that building a living human system that works well requires attention to both the task (i.e., the work of the meeting) and the process. "Process" is used to describe how people's attention comes to be focused, how energy/information gets used and how people relate in ways that are both satisfying and contributory to the work. At the beginning of SCT meetings, the first task is to identify a task and process leader. Often these are two different people, but one person can be both. In organizations, the team leader will often take the task leadership role and call for a volunteer to monitor process. We recommend that either leader, or a third individual also act as timekeeper. This role's responsibilities includes making sure the meeting begins and ends on time, and may involve monitoring how much time is spent on any one item. Finally, it is useful to identify a scribe who is responsible for summarizing the content of the meeting and also for recording next steps that emerge from discussions.

How to Begin a Meeting

SCT recognizes that the management of the transition into a meeting is important because it sets the conditions for the work to be done. At the beginning of meetings, SCT highlights the transition people must make from whatever has been occupying them before the meeting to a clear, direct focus on an articulated goal for the work of the meeting. SCT calls this "crossing the boundary" into work. Typically the process leader takes the lead in managing this transition. The shift from outside the meeting to inside orients everyone to focus on the work of the meeting and to let go of any competing agendas and responsibilities for the time of the meeting. Another way of conceptualizing this transition across the boundary into the meeting is that each person moves from their individual focus to seeing themselves as part of a functional system, where people act and interact in the service of the goal of the meeting. SCT calls this the "member" role (as distinct from one's personal agenda), where one focuses one's behavior and interactions in a way that facilitates the flow of information and supports the work and goals of the meeting.

The process leader begins focusing team members on transitioning into being a part of the system by asking if "anyone has a distraction?" (Agazarian, 1997). This is the opportunity for meeting participants to let each other know their other competing priorities or if they will need to keep their cell phones on or expect to leave early, etc. Occasionally the distraction will relate to a personal issue, like a sick child or a sleepless night. When the distractions are personal, the person has the opportunity to let others know of their personal circumstance or not and often feels relief and is able to focus on the meeting.

More often distractions relate to competing priorities—a customer, a deliverable, etc.—that produce conflicts between being at the meeting and performing an important task. Making these conflicts explicit enables the person to consciously choose how to set their priorities—whether to attend to the issue that is distracting them, or whether they want to deliberately shift their focus to the work of the meeting. This sets a norm of gathering everyone's energy and focus as part of preparing the system to work. It also legitimizes the inevitable conflicts people feel by addressing them directly. Asking people to make a decision about where they want to direct their energy and whether they want to move from their individual concerns to being a part of the meeting system highlights the importance of the meeting. For example, at a CEO roundtable, Frank announces to his colleagues that he is on-call regarding the unforeseen in the visit of an important international customer. Members understand, adjust their norms to make room for the exception, and are prepared for the possibility of Frank stepping out to answer his cell phone.

Goal

Once people are present and ready to work, the task leader orients the team to the meeting goals, both long and short term. The leader reviews the purpose of the meeting and places the meeting's goals and tasks within the larger organizational context. The task leader then names people that are absent and late and conveys the reason for their absence or lateness. In this way a norm is established for individuals taking accountability for keeping the team aware of their reasons for not being present. Once this is done, the leader can naturally shift to building the meeting's agenda. With the exception of weekly tactical meetings, it is always a good idea to circulate and build an agenda before the meeting (*Meetings Matter*, 1999). The leader hands out a finalized agenda at this point, noting any changes as needed.

The objectives of the "beginning of meetings" section are met when people are present, available for work and the goals of the current meeting and the larger context for the work are clear. Table I describes the goals of a group leader at the beginning of the meeting. Among the tasks inherent to the group leader position is the assignment of group members to different roles needed during the meeting, including the task and process leader roles. Table II describes the duties of a task leader and a process leader at the beginning of the meeting.

Table I
Goals in the Beginning of the Meeting

Goal	What needs to be done by the group leader
Fill Leadership Roles	Designate a task leader
	Designate a process leader
	Designate a timekeeper
	Designate a scribe
Set the structure for work	Get people ready and available to work
	Work to get the goal as clear as possible
	Circulate the agenda

Table II
Summary of Each Leader's Job at the Beginning of Meetings

Task Leader

- Structure the meeting
- Start the meeting on time
- Clarify the meeting's authority for task
- Name and explain absences of meeting participants
- Establish structure and hold functional norms
- Watch boundaries (cell phones on vibrate, etc.)
- Role clarifications and delegation: task, process, next steps
- Organize the agenda

Process Leader

- Ensure people are ready to work
- Orient move from person or social role to "member" role
- Orient late members (opportunity for group to review)
- Name who is absent and why at the beginning of the meeting

Middle: Doing the Work

The beginning of the meeting sets the foundation for work by building the system conditions that facilitate the work happening. If all has gone well, leadership roles are in place, people are present and their energy is focused on the task/goal of the meeting. The middle of the meeting is when the work gets done.

Prioritizing the agenda often marks the transition from the beginning of the meeting into the actual work. Once the agenda is prioritized, the work on each item can begin. Often each item will be represented or summarized by a member of the group. If not, the task leader orients the group to the agenda item.

Roles That Get the Work Done

The task leader's job is to make sure the goal of the discussion is clear and the work stays on task. The process leader's job is to watch that the group has enough information coming in that the work can get done and not too much that the group gets bogged down. Clearly these roles may overlap, and it is often very useful for the task and process leader to confer with each other.

During the middle section of a meeting, meeting participants are in one of two roles: either as a sponsor of a section of the agenda or as a participant in the discussion. Participants' responsibility is to voice their perspectives on the subject, and, if needed, on how the discussion is progressing. For example, if you are a participant and the leader makes a statement you disagree with, your disagreement is useful information for the team. It is vital to the effective decision making of the meeting that the team hears all the perspectives. Finding a way to voice concerns is crucial and part of each participant's responsibility. Similarly, if participants find their minds wandering during the discussion, it is their responsibility to let their colleagues know and to ask if others are also struggling to stay tuned in as well.

Sponsors take responsibility for agenda items. As a sponsor of an agenda item, you take the lead and orient the group to the agenda item. Effective sponsorship requires advance planning and clarity about what must be accomplished in the meeting to move the issue forward. Generally we suggest a sponsor provide at least these five orienting pieces of information:

- Identify the issue
- Provide relevant background
- Update on current status
- Identify your goal for the meeting; Do you want the team to provide input, to brainstorm, or make a decision/recommendation? (Trey, 1996)
- Immediate next step

Sponsors can quickly disseminate this information using the Issue Paper Format (see appendix 1). The Issue Paper is a one-page format to quickly summarize an agenda item and focus the team's discussion. Then, the sponsor facilitates the portion of the meeting so the goals are met and the agenda item can be moved forward.

SCT Tools for Getting Work Done

We are highlighting four specific SCT methods that are especially helpful in the work of the meeting:

- Taking the noise out of talk.
- Functional subgrouping whenever a difference or conflict arises.
- Developing shared criteria for each decision that needs to be made.
- Reducing speculations and negative predictions and keeping the discussion based in reality.

1. Taking the noise out of talk. This job falls to the process leader. The process leader keeps an eye on the communication process as the group does its work, with particular attention to lowering the common sources of noise in human communication: ambiguity or vagueness, redundancy and contradiction. Vagueness can be changed by asking members to be more specific. Redundancy can be reduced by reminding the group to get to the bottom line. Similarly, redundancy is weakened by introducing the choice (SCT calls this the "fork in the road") between explaining what is already known and the team's exploring aspects of the issue that are not yet clear (Agazarian, 1997; Gantt & Agazarian, 2004). This distinction also allows team members to identify when a discussion is an unnecessary rehash of what is known versus when it covers new territory that will help move the issue forward.

Changing contradictions will be discussed in the following section on modifying conflict. SCT takes for granted that the manner in which someone presents a viewpoint has a greater influence on a discussion than the specific content contained within the viewpoint. Similarly, the less noise a person uses when communicating, the higher likelihood there is that the communication will be effective. One way of classifying the productivity of a communication is to introduce meeting participants to the concepts of Red, Yellow and Green communications (Simon & Agazarian, 1967). People innately know the difference between red communications where no communication happens; yellow communications where whether the message comes through depends on whether the overall communication is red or green; and green communications where the message is clearly sent and delivered. Simon and Agazarian (1967) developed these concepts as part of a communications model which codifies communications based on whether or not these communications approach or avoid problem-solving. The model, SAVI (Systematic Analysis of Verbal Interactions), is further described in Chapter 6 in this book.

2. Resolve conflicts and work with differences. When Swiss watchmakers heard of an idea for a digital watch, they reluctantly funded a research group to explore the idea. The Swiss team was hampered by a lack of cooperation by the consortium of watch companies that funded the project—and the Japanese profited greatly from their failure to embrace the possibility of a different way of keeping time (Stephens & Dennis, 2000).

This is an excellent example of the challenge for human systems in relating to information that is too different from a commonly accepted perspective. All too often, the "new" information is discarded. Janus (1972) described a similar process in his understanding of "group think" where a group begins to believe its own internal logic despite the existence of contradictory evidence. In that instance, reality itself is skewed and decision-making occurs without the benefit of innovative thinking. Equally disturbing, important information brought to a meeting by someone reviled by the team will be dismissed on the basis of the messenger, without an assessment of the strategic import of the information.

SCT has developed functional subgrouping as a disciplined method for managing differences so they are used to benefit the work, rather than being ignored or becoming a source of contention. Functional subgrouping involves giving each side of a controversial topic its own conversational space where it can be developed. Functional subgrouping is appropriate whenever there is a decision to be made in which there are seemingly incompatible points of view in the group. Functional subgrouping also interrupts the "fix it" mentality of squelching disagreement as quickly as possible and instead introduces a focus on developing information before jumping to premature decisions. For the task leader, it is important to make sure there is enough time in the agenda to use functional subgrouping to explore an issue.

Functional subgrouping is an alternative to the contradiction of "yes, but" communications. For example, Don proposes a new procedure for tracking the agenda, and Sue responds: "Yes, but we already have addressed the issues about how we organize our agenda and revisiting it would take too much time." Don: "Yes, but this would help us work more efficiently." Sue: "Yes, maybe it would, but I think the time would be better spent otherwise."

As you can see, "yes, buts" provoke "yes, buts". Functional subgrouping provides an alternative and legitimizes both perspectives contained in the "Yes, but." The discussion is organized so first one perspective is explored, e.g., the "yes," and then the other side, the "but." In this way both sides are unpacked and understood, rather than each side polarizing the other.

The object of functional subgrouping is to allow individuals with like-minded perspectives on an issue to build on each other without opposition, while the others "listen in." The signal to begin subgrouping occurs when one person presents an idea about a subject and asks, "Anyone else see it this way?" In SCT-style meetings, this phrase signals to those that want to build on the perspective to participate and those that disagree or do not have a viewpoint to remain silent and listen. If a participant with a different perspective speaks up at this point, that person is asked to wait until those with similar viewpoints are ready to hear the other perspectives in the room. As the first side pauses, those who hold alternative perspectives are encouraged to join and talk together. In this sequencing of the discussion, first one side and then the other explores their views in the climate of similarity. As the discussion continues, more often than not, a bridge or integration between the two sides begins to emerge. This integration is often experienced as unexpected and surprising and usually results in richer, more textured decision-making. For example, in the above dialogue, functional subgrouping would be introduced as follows:

> Don: I think we are ready for an off-site meeting.
> Sue: Yes, but we already have too much work to do.
> Process leader: So we have the two sides of the issue. Sue, which do you want to discuss, your yes—that a retreat is a good idea or your "but," that is your hesitation about a retreat?
> Sue: Hmm, I'm really much clearer about my hesitations, I'd like to focus there.
> Process leader: OK, so since Don began the conversation with his interest in an off-site meeting, let's hear from Don and those who see us as ready for off-site, and about their criteria for why an off-site meeting would be a good idea now.
> Don: One of my criteria is that we never seem to get at the underlying issues in this hour-long meeting, I think if we had more time. Anybody else interested in the off-site idea?
> Terry: I am, and like you, Don I think we need a bigger block of time to sort out what gets in the way of implementation. Also, we spend more time being thoughtful about doing pre-work for an off-site and I think that will help us in solving this problem.

Thomas: I think so too, in these shorter meetings, we get bogged down and don't have time to step back and see the bigger picture.
Jim: As you're talking, I'm getting clearer on the other side of this, that this is not the time for an off-site. Are you finished so we can discuss the other side?
Don: Not just yet, I'd like to finish a bit more of the pluses for an off-site meeting.

This process asks meeting participants to be disciplined about when and how they present their perspectives on issues. It also interrupts the contentiousness that develops as members try to convert others to their side. Instead of diverting the energy into conversion attempts, all of the attention at the meeting is focused on exploring a particular perspective more fully.

3. Developing shared criteria for each decision that needs to be made. In decision-making conversations, SCT emphasizes the importance of initially developing an agreed upon set of criteria to be used for the decision-making. Discussions about criteria allow the participants to understand where there are points of agreement and where the true differences lie. These discussions clarify the basis for decision-making. For example, in the conversation about the off-site meeting the crucial difference between those who wanted the off-site now and those who didn't was not about the need for an off-site meeting, but rather the timing of the off-site. Essentially, the issue became whether the off-site meeting should occur before or after the organization implemented a new financial system. Those that were involved with the implementation and knew of the new financial systems capabilities felt that the kind of data the system could provide where worth waiting for. Those that did not believe the off-site meeting could wait believed that the information currently available was sufficient. This became a testable criteria and a small group made up of both perspectives offered to come back with a recommendation.

4. Reducing speculations and negative predications and keeping the discussion based in reality. We've already mentioned that human systems can easily detach themselves from reality. SCT introduces several techniques that help human systems redirect their attention from "irreality" to reality. SCT, building on Lewin (1951), identifies three classes of irreality: irreality that is about the past, the present and the future. In each case, the job of the process leader is to identify the irrealities and alert the team to them so the team can begin to correct itself and get back in sync with reality.

People are out of reality about the past when they communicate a much-repeated story about the past. Stories entertain and often make a point yet they rarely help the people in its system clarify reality.

When people are out of reality in the present they are making assumptions or speculations about how other people are thinking and feeling. So for example, if someone says, "I know what you are thinking," they are not in reality unless they have the ability to read other people's minds 100% of the time. SCT calls these kinds of assumptions "mind reads." The leader can counter "mind reads" by simply checking their accuracy with the mind being "read." The goal of this is not to embarrass any individual, but to reduce the effect of processes that push the group further out of sync with reality.

Finally, negative predictions or speculations about the future, which we've previously mentioned, are examples of being out of reality about the future. The leader can ask the individual to bring the information they are withholding into reality by getting the individual to recognize the irreality. Again, the goal is to reduce the influence of processes that keep information out of the group and, consequently, further away from reality.

To summarize, as the conversation unfolds during this middle section of the meeting, leaders track the system as well as the work of the meeting. Table III, below, is a summary of some of the questions leaders are asking to themselves:

Table III

Questions in the Leaders' Minds during Middle of Meeting
• Are differences getting explored and supported as information for the system, or are differences getting avoided or glossed over?
• Does the structure support differences coming in, or in contrast is the agenda so tightly structured that there is little room for differences or new ideas?
• Is the meeting structure helping the group to work?
• Is the goal of the meeting clear to everyone?
• How does the information cross the boundary into the meeting, and when it gets in does it get taken up in the meeting?
• How does the information get used, toward or away from the goal? Does the system work to clarify or obscure it?

The leader's job is to monitor these dimensions and to intervene so the system's structure facilitates the flow of information, the emergence of differing perspectives and is focused on staying in reality.

End: Transition from Working to Reviewing

The goal of the end of a meeting is to bring closure to the work. To this end, SCT asks participants to review the accomplishments of the meeting through identifying the next steps and then reflecting on the experience of the meeting. The process of identifying the next steps includes both a review of the meeting's work and a setting of the implementation plans. Reviewing the meeting process provides individuals with the chance to improve on the way the meeting happened.

Next Steps

The task leader's job is to structure the close of the meeting so the objectives are achieved. The task leader bridges from the previous section of the meeting to the conclusion by reviewing the work accomplished during the meeting and suggests (often with the group's help) the outstanding work still remaining. This begins to set the agenda for the next meeting. Once the team has transitioned from doing the work to planning for the next steps, the leader or a designee who has been keeping track of next steps identified during the meeting, reads the list. Participants have either signed up to steward a next step by clearly committing to what they will do and by when or the team recognizes a need to decide how to manage that next step.

Meeting Review

When the next steps are clear, the process leader asks the meeting participants to think back over the meeting and critique it. SCT does this by asking for any "surprises, learnings, satisfactions, dissatisfactions or discoveries" from the meeting. This kind of review surfaces any difficulties (dissatisfactions) so they can be addressed in the next meeting. Whenever a dissatisfying aspect is identified, the process leader asks the participant who is dissatisfied to also identify what they can do differently in the next meeting so they are more satisfied. This shifts dissatisfactions away from complaining to learning about what the participant him/herself can do differently, not about what others needed to do. The review also highlights the successes in a way that the team will be able to deliberately replicate them. Finally, this kind of review helps meeting participants prepare to shift gears from this meeting to whatever comes next.

Although it is tempting to bypass this final element of systems work, we strongly suggest incorporating it into the meeting agenda. For a system to develop it must be able to learn and communicate about what worked and didn't work. This is how systems develop a reflective capacity. Instead of frustrations coming out in the hallways, in ways that are difficult to address, they can come out during the meeting in a way that the team will be able to address them.

Conclusion

From a systems perspective, meetings are the organizational hub for transferring information. Transferring information through two-sided effective communication is the energy that fuels the work of organizations. To the extent that meetings work effectively and participants have a good feeling for their work, the entire organization benefits. In this chapter, we have introduced a meeting structure using the principles and methods of SCT. These methods do two things at once: they get the work done and they build the system.

How the system functions governs how work gets done and what work gets done. From our experience with a range of different companies and organizations, using SCT methods has enabled meetings to go from draining to exciting with the result that members consistently work more productively, have greater satisfaction in their work, and increase the flow of information that is the vitality in all living human systems. Using SCT methods not only helps the work happen, it also develops a systems perspective for managers, leaders and participants that decreases the tendency to personalize. Finally, SCT enables already skilled leaders to use their existing meeting skills more effectively by expanding their perspective to seeing and building the system inherent in all meetings.

Appendix 1—The Issue Paper[2]

The issue paper approach is a straightforward and effective way to present an agenda item that needs to be addressed and resolved. The format of the issue paper helps to organize thinking about the factors contributing to the problem and helps to clarify and identify the work of the team on that issue.

<u>Issue:</u> Brief description of the issue

<u>Background:</u> What factors/events have brought this issue forward? Why is this coming up at this time?

<u>Current Status:</u> What is the current practice of how to deal with the issue?
Detailed description of how the problem is dealt with currently and what the implications are.

<u>Recommendations:</u> What do you want the team to do at this meeting about this issue?

<u>Next Step:</u> What steps need to be taken to implement a change?

---

2. Our thanks to Kathy Criswell who first introduced us to the Issue Paper.

About the Authors

Yvonne Agazarian, Ed.D., FAGPA, CGP, is the developer of a theory of living human systems and its systems-centered practice and the founder of the Systems-Centered Training and Research Institute. She lives in Philadelphia and teaches and consults internationally. In 1997 she received the Group Psychologist of the year award from the American Psychological Association "for her involvement in research, publication, teaching and training. She exemplifies the finest in scholarship in the discipline of psychology...she has contributed to expanding our knowledge of the boundaries between clinical and social psychology...Her considerable body of work illustrates the highest blend of creativity and learning."

Claudia Byram, Ph.D., has been working with SAVI since 1975, and with systems-centered theory and methods since their inception. She has been an active participant in developing SAVI training and coding manuals, in teaching SAVI to people in business, education and clinical fields for 25 years. She is a psychotherapist practicing in Philadelphia, PA, a licensed systems-centered practitioner, continues to teach and train both SAVI and SCT, and is part of the management group of the Systems-Centered Training and Research Institute.

Fran Carter, LSW, is a licensed systems-centered practitioner, and a trainer and organizational consultant. In her clinical practice, she works with individuals, couples and groups. In her consulting practice, she works with all aspects of staff and organizational development, conflict resolution and change. She is a senior SCT trainer and conducts foundation, intermediate and advanced trainings in the United States and Europe. She is a founding member of the Systems-Centered Training and Research Institute where she is part of the management group and serves as mentor to the organization.

Susan Gantt, Ph.D., CGP, ABPP, is the Director of the Systems-Centered Training and Research Institute. She works as a psychologist in private practice in Atlanta and part-time for Emory University School of Medicine. She is a licensed systems-centered practitioner, a diplomat in group psychology, and trains and consults internationally in the systems-centered approach. She co-authored the book *Autobiography of a Theory* with Yvonne Agazarian and has published in the journals *Organizational Analysis, Group Dynamics,* and *Journal of Counseling Psychology.*

Dorothy Gibbons, LCSW, is a psychotherapist and organizational consultant in private practice in Philadelphia, PA. She is the co-author of *Encountering Bigotry: Befriending Projecting People in Everyday Life* and *Working with Victims: Being Empathic Helpers.* She directed a program for Juvenile Sex Offenders for six years, and has worked with victims and offenders of sexual abuse for over ten years. Dorothy is a graduate of Bryn Mawr College Graduate School of Social Work and Social Research. She is a member of the steering group for the Systems-Centered Training and Research Institute.

Joan Hemenway, D.Min., is a chaplain supervisor certified by the Association for Clinical Pastoral Education. For the past 30 years, her focus has been on the training of clergy and seminarians in programs of clinical pastoral education (CPE) offered in hospitals, nursing homes and mental health facilities. Her book entitled *Inside the Circle: A Historical and Practical Inquiry Concerning Process Groups in Clinical Pastoral Education* is used in CPE programs throughout the country. She is currently President-Elect of the Association for Clinical Pastoral Education.

Jane Maloney, MA, earned her Masters degree in organizational psychology at Columbia University and is an organization effectiveness consultant and executive coach in New York City. A frequent speaker and workshop leader, she has offered leadership, management and team development programs that have allowed organizations to dramatically improve productivity and profitability. Her clients include Ernst & Young, Merrill Lynch, and Lucent Technologies, as well as not-for-profit organizations.

Claude Marchessault, MA, is a founder and senior consultant at Strategic Leadership Group, Inc. where he assists CEO's and BOD's in addressing the challenges of developing leadership teams that can lead leaders, confront reality, build strategic thinking capacity, align culture to shared core values, and design organizational processes that deliver results. In this role and as an executive mediator, an executive coach, and facilitator of monthly strategic thinking roundtable for CEO's, he contributes to the application of systems theory to business and organizational life.

Edward Marshall, Ph.D., is the Head of Greene Street Friends School and an adjunct assistant professor in the Graduate School of Education of the University of Pennsylvania. He took his undergraduate training in history and received his graduate degree in physics. He is particularly interested in applications of systems-centered training to educational settings. He lives with his family near Philadelphia in the United States.

Irene McHenry, Ph.D., is the Executive Director of Friends Council on Education. She was founding Head of Delaware Valley Friends School, a co-founder of Greenwood Friends School and Fielding Graduate Institute's doctoral program in Educational Leadership. She is a board member for Council for American Private Education, Haverford College, Friends Center Corporation, and Friends Education Fund. She co-authored *Readings on Quaker Pedagogy* with Fremon, Hammond and Starmer; *Governance Handbook for Friends Schools* with Hoopes; and co-edited *Schooled in Diversity* with Macpherson and Sweeney-Denham.

Chris McIlroy, MSC, is an organizational psychologist certified by the Swedish National Board of Health and Welfare. He has been actively involved in developing SCT in Sweden. He is a board member and part owner of Sandahl Partners Sweden. He works with developing small working groups and with managerial coaching with companies in Sweden, Europe and the US.

Verena Murphy, LSW, was born and raised in Switzerland, where she obtained a public school teaching degree. After moving to the United States in 1977, she worked for 20 years in community and geriatric mental health in San Francisco and Philadelphia. She has been training in SCT since 1995, and is currently at Case Western Reserve University, Department of Organizational Behavior, writing her dissertation. Her research interests are in higher education and the application of SCT in organizations.

Richard M. O'Neill, Ph.D., FAClinP, CGP, is Director of SCT Training at the State University of New York Upstate Medical University. He is a former President of the New York State Psychological Association (NYSPA). His successful NYSPA presidential initiative, affiliating with a national labor union to deal with managed care, was featured on the front-page of the New York Times. He has 200+ television appearances on psychology and a 1976 Student Academy Award for the documentary *What The Notes Say*.

Caroline Packard, JD, is the Change and Conflict Response Specialist at Philadelphia Yearly Meeting, serving 105 Quaker congregations. In addition, as the principal of Packard Process Consulting, she helps boards, nonprofits, family businesses and partnerships resolve conflicts, plan collaboratively, and develop policies for growth; and provides coaching and mediation services to individuals. A former corporate litigator, she has trained hundreds of mediators, and is a co-designer of Friends Conflict Resolution Programs' nationally known mediation-training courses.

Anita Simon, Ed.D., is a psychologist in private practice in Philadelphia, specializing in work with couples and individuals. She is the co-developer, with Yvonne Agazarian, of the SAVI System for Analyzing Verbal Interaction. She was editor of *Mirrors for Behaviors*, a 17 volume encyclopedia of observation systems. She founded *Classroom Observation Newsletter* (currently the *Journal of Classroom Interaction*). She has been writing and publishing about SAVI since 1965, and delivering workshops at professional conferences and for therapists and the general public since 1968.

Beulah Trey, Ph.D., is Senior Manager at CFAR (The Center for Applied Research, Inc.), a management consulting firm that combines a strong social-science tradition with business experience. She co-leads CFAR's Leadership Transition and Succession practice area, manages the family business specialty area, and works with leaders and teams on strategic objectives. A licensed psychologist, her research focus is the relationship between trust, conflict and institutional effectiveness. She received her Ph.D. from the University of Pennsylvania and her BA from Swarthmore College.

References

Agazarian, Y.M. (1967). *Using the force field in systems-centered leadership.* Unpublished paper.

Agazarian, Y.M. (1968). *A theory of verbal behavior and information transfer.* Unpublished doctoral dissertation, Temple University, Philadelphia, PA.

Agazarian, Y.M. (1969). A theory of verbal behavior and information transfer. *Classroom Interaction Newsletter, 4*(2), 22-33.

Agazarian, Y.M. (1972). A system for analyzing verbal behavior (SAVI) applied to staff training in Milieu treatment. *Devereux Schools Forum, 1*, 1-32.

Agazarian, Y.M. (1986). Applications of Lewin's life space concept to the individual and group-as-a-whole systems in psychotherapy. In E. Stivers & S. Wheelan (Eds.), *The Lewin legacy.* New York: Springer-Verlag.

Agazarian, Y.M. (1992). Contemporary theories of group psychotherapy: A systems approach to the group-as-a-whole. *International Journal of Group Psychotherapy, 42*(2), 177-203.

Agazarian, Y.M. (1993). Reframing the group-as-a-whole. In T. Hugg, N. Carson, & R. Lipgar (Eds.), *Changing group relations.* Jupiter, FL: A.K. Rice Institute.

Agazarian, Y.M. (1994). The phases of development and the systems-centered group. In M. Pines & V. Schermer (Eds.), *Ring of fire: Primitive object relations and affect in group psychotherapy.* London: Routledge, Chapman & Hall.

Agazarian, Y.M. (1996). An up-to-date guide to the theory, constructs and hypotheses of a theory of living human systems and its systems-centered practice. *The SCT Journal, 1*(1), 3-12.

Agazarian, Y.M. (1997). *Systems-centered therapy for groups.* New York: Guilford.

Agazarian, Y.M. (1999). Phases of development in the systems-centered group. *Small Group Research, 30* (1), 82-107.

Agazarian, Y.M. (2001). *A systems-centered approach to inpatient group psychotherapy.* London and Philadelphia: Jessica Kingsley.

Agazarian, Y.M. (2003). *Roles.* Unpublished paper.

Agazarian, Y.M. & Gantt, S.P. (2000). *Autobiography of a theory.* London: Jessica Kingsley.

Agazarian, Y.M. & Gantt, S.P. (2003). Phases of group development: Systems-centered hypotheses and their implications for research and practice. *Group Dynamics: Theory, Research and Practice, 7*(3), 238-252.

Agazarian, Y.M. & Gantt, S.P. (2004). *Leading edges in systems-centered theory and practice.* Paper presented at the Systems-Centered Training Conference, Atlanta, GA.

Agazarian, Y.M. & Gantt, S.P. (2005). The systems perspective. In S. Wheelan (Ed.), *Handbook of group research and practice.* Newbury Park, CA: Sage Publications.

Agazarian, Y.M. & Janoff, S. (1993). Systems theory and small groups. In I. Kaplan & B. Sadock (Eds.), *Comprehensive textbook of group psychotherapy,* 3rd edition (pp. 33-44). Maryland: Williams & Wilkins, Division of Waverly.

Agazarian, Y.M. & Peters, R. (1981). *The visible and invisible group.* London: Karnac.

Agazarian, Y.M. & Philibossian, B. (1998). A theory of living human systems as an approach to leadership of the future with examples of how it works. In E. Klein, F. Gabelnick & P. Herr (Eds.), *The psychodynamics of leadership* (pp. 127-160). Madison, CT: Psychosocial Press.

Amidon, E. & Flanders, N. A. (1961). The effects of direct and indirect teacher influence on dependent-prone students learning geometry. *Journal of Educational Research, 35,* 2.

Amidon E. & Simon A. (April 1967). Teacher pupil interaction. *Review of Educational Research, 35,* 130-39.

Asquith, G. (n.d.). *Guidelines for Lebenslauf.* Moravian Seminary, Bethlehem, PA.

Association for Clinical Pastoral Education. (2003). *ACPE Annual Report.* Decatur, GA.

Association for Clinical Pastoral Education. (2005). *ACPE Draft of 2005 Standards.* Retrieved from www.acpe.edu.

Bennis, W. (1989). *Why leaders can't lead: The unconscious conspiracy.* San Francisco: Jossey-Bass.

Bennis, W.G. & Shepard, H.A. (1956). A theory of group development. *Human Relations, 9*(4), 415-437.

Bertalanffy, L. von. (1968). *General system theory: Foundations, development, applications.* New York: George Braziller.

Bion, W.R. (1959). *Experiences in groups.* London: Tavistock.

Bridger, H. (1946). The Northfield experiment. *Bulletin of the Menninger Clinic, 10*(3), 71-76.

Bridger, H. (1990). Courses and working conferences as transitional learning institutions. In E. Trist, H. Murray et al (Eds.), *The social engagement of social science: A Tavistock anthology, Vol. I: The socio-psychological perspective.* (pp. 221-245). Baltimore: University of Pennsylvania Press.

Browne, R.M. (1977). *Patient and professional interaction and its relationship to patients' health status and frequent use of health services.* Unpublished doctoral dissertation. University of Toronto.

Dewey, J. (1916). *Democracy and education: An introduction to the philosophy of education.* New York: Macmillan.

Edmondson, A.C. (1999). Psychological safety and behavior in work teams. *Administrative Science Quarterly, 44,* 350-383.

Edmondson, A.C. (2002). The local and variegated nature of learning in organizations: A group-level perspective. *Organization Science, 13*(2), 128-146.

Faith and Practice (1972). Philadelphia Yearly Meeting of the Religious Society of Friends.

Fellows, J. (1996). SAVI training for a small team in conflict. *Systems-Centered Training News,* 4(1), 15.

Festinger, L. (1957). *A theory of cognitive dissonance.* Evanston, IL: Row, Peterson.

Flanders, N.A. (1962). Using interaction analysis in the in-service training of teachers. *Journal of Experimental Education,* 30(4), 313-16.

Flanders, N.A. (1965). Teacher influence, pupil attitudes and achievement. U.S. Department of Health, Education and Welfare, Office of Education. *Cooperative Research Monograph No. 12.*

Flanders, N.A. & Simon, A. (1969). Teacher effectiveness. In R.L. Ebel (Ed.), *Encyclopedia of educational research* (pp. 507-582). New York: Macmillan.

Gallagher, J. J. (1966). A topic classification system in the analysis of BSCS concept presentations. *Classroom Interaction Newsletter,* 2(2), 12-16.

Gantt, S.P. & Agazarian, Y.M. (2004). Systems-centered emotional intelligence: Beyond individual systems to organizational systems. *Organizational Analysis,* 12(2), 147-169.

Gardner, H. (1999, February). Who owns intelligence. *The Atlantic Monthly.*

Goleman, D. (1998). *Working with emotional intelligence.* New York: Bantam Books.

Grant, M. & Cavanaugh, M. (2004). Toward a profession of coaching: Sixty-five years of progress and challenges for the future. *International Journal of Evidence Based Coaching and Mentoring,* 2(1), 1-16.

Hall, C.E. (1992). *Head and heart: The story of the clinical pastoral education movement.* Decatur, GA: Journal of Pastoral Care Publications, Inc.

Harvey, J.B. (1974). The Abilene paradox: The management of agreement. *Organizational Dynamics,* 3(1), 63-80.

Hemenway, J.E. (1996). *Inside the circle: A historical and practical inquiry into process groups in clinical pastoral education.* Decatur: Journal of Pastoral Care Publications, Inc.

Howard, A. & Scott, R.A. (1974). A proposed framework for the analysis of stress in the human organism. *Journal of Applied Behavioral Science, 10,* 141-160.

Hughes, H. (1984). Listen to your meeting's message. *Successful Meetings, 33*(2), 62-68.

Hunt, W. (1987). *Teaching and learning in the affective domain: A review of literature.* Olympia, WA: Office of the State Superintendent of Public Instruction. PPIC Document Reproduction Series # ED 288871.

International Coaching Federation. (2004). Code of Ethics. Retrieved January 3, 2005 from http://www.coachfederation.org/ethics/code_ethics.asp

Janus, I.L. (1972). *Victims of groupthink.* Boston: Houghton Mifflin.

Kempner, M. (2004, October 10). Gerald Grinstein's hire wire act: Delta's future in the balance as CEO struggles to bring off rescue mission. *The Atlanta Journal-Constitution.*

Korzybski, A. (1948). *Science and sanity: An introduction to non-Aristotelian systems and general semantics.* Lakeville, CT: International Non-Aristotelian Library, Institute of General Semantics.

Lee, K.S. (2003). *A prolegomena to multicultural competencies in clinical pastoral education.* Unpublished paper.

Lewin, K. (1951). *Field theory in social science.* New York: Harper & Row.

MacKinnon, J.R. (1984). Health professionals' patterns of communication: Cross-purpose or problem solving? *Journal of Allied Health, 4,* 3-12.

McCluskey, U. (2002a). *Training in goal-corrected empathic attunement: The process of affect regulation within the instinctive systems of care seeking and care giving.* Paper presented at the Systems-Centered Training Conference, Philadelphia, PA.

McCluskey, U. (2002b). The dynamics of attachment and systems-centered group psychotherapy. *Group Dynamics: Theory, Research and Practice 6*(2), 131-142.

McHenry, I. (2003). *The use of subgrouping as a dialogue method in educational classroom contexts: An action research study.* Paper presented at the Systems-Centered Training Conference, Philadelphia, PA.

Meetings Work: A guide to participative systems (CFAR Tool). (1999). Philadelphia, PA: CFAR, Inc.

Miller, J. (1978). *Living systems.* New York: McGraw-Hill.

Oppenheim, L. (1987). *Making meetings matter: A report to the 3M company* (CFAR Report). Philadelphia, PA: CFAR, Inc.

Parks, E. (2003). *Subgrouping and conflict management: A research update.* Paper presented at the Systems-Centered Training Conference, Philadelphia, PA.

Powell, E. (1972). Classroom climate, pupil intelligence and mechanical skills learning. *Classroom Interaction Newsletter, 8*(2), 18-20.

Reason, P. & Bradbury, H. (Eds.). (2000). *Handbook of action research.* Thousand Oaks, CA: Sage Publications.

Redfield, D. & Rousseau, E. (1981). A meta analysis of experimental research on teacher questioning behavior. *Review of Educational Research 51*(2), 237-45.

Rowe, M. (1986). Wait time: Slowing down may be a way of speeding up. *Journal of Teacher Education, 37*(1), 43-50.

Sagor, R. (1991). What project LEARN reveals about collaborative action research. *Educational Leadership, 48*(6), 6.

Sandberg, J. (2004, September 29). Cubicle Culture. *The Wall Street Journal,* p. B1.

Senge, P. (1990). *The fifth discipline.* New York: Doubleday.

Shannon, C. E. & Weaver, W. (1964). *The mathematical theory of communication.* Urbana, IL: University of Illinois Press.

Simon, A. (1967). *Patterns of verbal behavior in favored and non-favored classes.* Unpublished doctoral dissertation. Temple University.

Simon, A. (1993). Using SAVI for couples' therapy. *Journal of Family Psychotherapy, 4,* 39-62.

Simon, A. (1996a). SAVI and individual SCT therapy. *The SCT Journal: Systems-Centered Theory and Practice, 1,* 65-71.

Simon, A. (1996b). Behavior hopping with SAVI. *Systems-Centered Training News, 4*(2), 22-24.

Simon, A. (1996c). SAVI mind-read alert. *Systems-Centered Training News, (4)*1, 11-12.

Simon, A. & Agazarian, Y.M. (1967). SAVI: Sequential analysis of verbal interaction. In Simon, A. & Boyer, E.G. (Eds.), *Mirrors for behavior: An anthology of classroom observation instruments.* Philadelphia: Research for Better Schools.

Simon A. & Agazarian, Y.M. (2000). SAVI—The system for analyzing verbal interaction. In A.P. Beck & C.M Lewis (Eds.), *The process of group psychotherapy: Systems for analyzing change* (pp.357-380). Washington, D.C.: American Psychological Association.

Stephens, C. & Dennis, M. (2000). Engineering time: Inventing the electronic wristwatch. *British Journal for the History of Science, 33,* 477-497.

Sturdevant, K.S. (1991). *A pilot study of intrapersonal and interpersonal process as measured on the experiencing scale and the sequential analysis of verbal interaction (SAVI).* Unpublished master's thesis. University of Iowa.

Taba, H. et al (1964). *Thinking in elementary school children.* San Francisco State College: United States Department of Health, Education, and Welfare, Office of Education, Cooperative Research Project No. 1574.

Trey, B. (1996) Managing interdependence on the unit. *Health Care Management Review, 21*(3), 72-82.

Trey, B. (2002a). *Participative decision making* (CFAR Tool). Philadelphia, PA: CFAR, Inc.

Trey, B. (2002b). *The changing leader role as teams develop or a team's journey from misery to mastery: The role of the leader.* Paper presented at the Systems-Centered Training Conference, Philadelphia, PA.

Weir, R. (1978). *Treatment and outcome as a function of staff-patient interaction.* Unpublished doctoral dissertation. University of Toronto.

Wheelan, S. (1994/2004). *Group processes: A developmental perspective.* Needham Heights, MA: Allyn & Bacon.

Witt, J. (1998). *Action research and ways of knowing. ELC 701 study guide.* The Fielding Institute. Retrieved from http://www.fielding.edu/private/elc/cur/.

Zimmerman, K.W. (1970). *Verbal classroom interaction and characteristics including self-actualization of home economics teachers.* Unpublished doctoral dissertation. Iowa State University, Ames, IA.